God-Soul Theory
For
The 21st Century

Edward Conklin Ph.D.

Edward Conklin

ISBN 978-0-9988338-1-1

Dedication

I dedicate this work to the young, who not told, usually have to find out the hard way. I also dedicate this work to those brave few through history who explored body and brain and faithfully went where truth led them; their words continue to ring true and resound through time.

Acknowledgments

I owe my biological life to my parents and family generations. My psychological and philosophical orientation to life I owe in great part to my teacher, Dr. Amiya Chakravarty (1901-1986). Though I do not know if he would agree with my views, I certainly owe him my heartfelt thanks for inspiring me to think more deeply about life and the human condition.

Published works by Edward Conklin Ph.D.

God-Soul Theory for the 21st Century. (2017). Amazon Kindle and CreateSpace.

Psychology of God and the Soul. (2016). Amazon Kindle and CreateSpace.

Meditations on God and the Soul. (2015). Amazon Kindle and CreateSpace.

A Brief Guide to God and the Soul. (2015). Amazon Kindle and CreateSpace.

In the Beginning: A New Theory of the First Religion. (2014). Amazon Kindle and CreateSpace.

Cosmos, God, and Soul. (2014). Amazon Kindle and CreateSpace.

From Tool-maker to God Maker. (2014). Amazon Kindle and CreateSpace.

Waves Rough and Smooth & the Deep Blue Sea. (2014). Amazon Kindle and CreateSpace.

Getting Back Into the Garden of Eden. (1998). University Press of America.

Introduction

What follows is a series of short essays on the topics of a monotheistic god and the human soul. Over half the population of the earth or some three to four billion humans, accept the monotheistic view of a first father god. Most monotheists are members of the religions of Judaism, Christianity, and Islam. A great many have no affiliation with organized religion but simply classify themselves as spiritual. Since the idea of a universal first father god is important to so many, it evokes a need to be investigated and better comprehended.

This work discusses what I call the God-Soul Theory. The theory advocates that a human-like god exists only subjectively and is not objectively real. A monotheistic first father god is a subjective way of identifying an unknown beginning and a way of orienting to what is good, caring, and protective of humans. The God-Soul Theory proposes that all gods, especially the monotheistic first father god of Middle East origin and Western culture is an artistic creation of the cerebral cortex of the human brain.

The God-Soul Theory further asserts that the human soul is real and yet, is not a shining divine presence within but is a triune forcible hunger for food, sex and reproduction, and aggression that forces life to live and survive. The soul is a continuation of the energy elements of the earth, and is a continuation of a cosmological force that moves the universe and ever exists on its own.

To have the opportunity to investigate the mystery of a monotheistic god and an animating soul, has been both a burden on personal time and also a joy. The perceiving, creating, and writing on these two topics has at various times served as a much more uplifting experience than any socially accepted and customarily sanctioned conversation, alcohol, drug high, orgasm, and caffeine stimulant.

God-Soul Theory

The God-Soul Theory advocates a view of partial-atheism. The theory consists of the basic tenet that a human-like god is subjectively real to some humans but is not objectively real. A monotheistic first father god is a subjective way of identifying an unknown beginning and an imaginary way of orienting to what is good, caring, and protective of humans. The first father god of monotheism is derived not from reasoning as suggested and accepted in the past but is rather a product of artistic imagining in an effort to know an unknown beginning of the environment and life.

The God-Soul Theory also advocates that since a human-like god is an expression of artistic imagining, a popularly vaunted human soul cannot have been made by and has nothing to do with a god. The animating soul is a continuation of the natural environment of energy and force and it is this that renders it resistant to destruction. The soul is a triune forcible hunger for food, sex and reproduction, and aggression that is resistant to destruction and therefore aids life to survive.

Puzzle

Life consists of numerous puzzles most difficult to solve. The practice of external observation (in contrast to the internal observation of body and brain functions of meditation) known as modern science, has solved many of the puzzles of life. The science of objective observation has found that life consists of various parts related to conditions of the environment. Science attempts to solve much of the puzzle of life by investigating, observing, and naming parts and functions, and also by theorizing where the parts of the environment and life have come from.

In contrast, the thinking of monotheism, the view there is a first father god of humankind, is that the parts of the environment and life did not assemble randomly and evolve over long eons of time but that there is an assembler who assembled the various forms of existence.

The early prescientific and popular explanation is that an intelligent first father god created the environment and life on earth. This is the view of monotheistic religions, mainly of Judaism, Christianity, and Islam.

Some individuals undertake the study of theology, the subjective knowledge of a first father god. Religious officials, rabbis, priests, ministers, and imams learn how to relate to an invisible first father, and how to appeal to and convince others that the god exists objectively. In reality, the notion of a first father god is a subjective way of identifying the origin of existence, and is an imagined way of obtaining care and protection during life and after death.

The unpredictable behaviors of a mostly unknown environment and living forms must have been intimidating to early humans. To exist is a risk and therefore humans need protection in life. Life is often puzzling and beset by both good and evil problems of living. To solve the puzzle of the problems of life and death, some humans imagine a first father god. A monotheistic god is portrayed as dictating commands, and if the commandments are followed, then humans will live a better and protected life.

However, a first father god cannot be depended upon to dispense care and provide protection in a reliable way, therefore humans must find ways to render care and protection for themselves. Humans need protection from the environment, so shelters are built. The need for protection from the environment and other life forms provokes some individuals to better comprehend reality experience. In the past some individuals became tool and weapon makers. Some became a shaman to explore and observe the environment, plants, animals, and other dimensions. Eventually modern empirical science developed and continues to progress and to protect humans.

Humans need protection from the environment, and from accidents and disease and so insurance companies are formed. Humans need protection in one's own neighborhood, so a police, legal system, and fire rescue is formed.

Humans need protection from humans in other countries, so a military is formed. Humans need protection from infection and injuries and so antibiotics and medical treatments are developed. Humans need protection from poverty so an economy is formed. Humans utilize the cerebral cortex of the brain to invent and innovate these beneficial developments.

Humans need protection from hunger, disease, poverty, ageing, and death. Therefore, some unthinking individuals exaggerate the beginning of existence and imagine it to be an exalted forefather, a human-like god. Only unthinking individuals seek protection by imagining the beginning to be a first father god who made the environment and life, and who can control existence, and can then save humans from harm and death.

What protects humans best is the cerebral cortex of the brain. The cerebral cortex reasons, it measures objects in space-time through transforming sensations into picture images of now, past, and future events. The cerebral cortex of the brain, especially in the past, and continuing as a cognitive artifact, ineffectively protects humans by imagining the existence of a first father god in a sequence of biological fathers.

Exaggeration

The English word exaggerate is derived from the Latin word exaggerare, meaning to heap up, to make greater, and to make a mound or pile of things. To exaggerate literally means to:

"Overstate, to increase or enlarge in size, to magnify, to go beyond the limits of what is true, and to represent as larger or greater, as more important or more successful, and more noticeable than is true."

A monotheistic first father god is an overstatement, an increase and enlargement of the origin of the environment and life to be human-like.

A first father god magnifies, makes the origin of existence overly important, larger, and more noticeable by imagining and going beyond the limits of what is true. Monotheistic humans piled many previous forefathers into one big untrue first father and exaggerated it to be a god.

A first father god is a subjective artistic use of words as a way of noticing human origin. Many are gullible enough to accept the artistic exaggeration of a first father god of goodness. The exaggerating of what is good for humans convincingly suggests how bad life really is. Frail humans struggle with often unrelenting circumstances and evils of the environment, other life forms, and fellow humans. Monotheistic believers band together in the imagined presence of a good first father god, and together agree to use their higher cerebral cortex to do what is good.

Exaggeration and acceptance of the origin of existence to be a first father god became a tradition that eventually developed into monotheism. Scattered randomly across the earth, churches, mosques, synagogues, and temples, stand as small beacons and places of good in a sea of many life evils. The monotheistic havens from evil tout the beginning of existence to be a good first father god.

The inward subjective ideation of good as a first father god, is projected outward to be an object that represents the higher cerebral cortex of the human brain, precisely where the idea originates. A monotheistic gathering is a way of locating good on a good and evil earth. The imagined idea of a first father god is the projective ability of the cerebral cortex of the human brain to identify its origin and to make higher choices of behavior. The ideation of a first father god serves to subjectively seek for and to identify what is good.

The monotheistic god identifies the beginning of life as a first father, and in so doing overlooks and discounts the supportive earth, and also ignores the genealogical progression of sexual reproduction.

A monotheistic first father imaginatively and clumsily represents where life comes from, the real supportive environment and the long biological line of sexual reproduction. Sexual force that produces individual life is a continuation of atom and electron energy elements of the earth, and the movement of life and the environment are related to a cosmological force that moves the universe and that ever exists on its own.

Artistic Story

A monotheistic first father god is an artistic imagined explanation for the existence of the environment and life. An intelligent first father is the poor attempt of the cerebral cortex of the Semitic brain circa 700 BCE to find the location of its own origin. Having little objective evidence to rely on aside from the biological line of human fathers, the biblical authors relied on the ability for subjective imagination. The artistic ability to imagine is what created the story of a first father god who walks in the Garden in the cool of the day. (Genesis 3:8)

Who is the narrator and witness to the events of the biblical story of Genesis? Surely no other humans existed. The third person is none other than the narrating verbal artist, the story teller. The Genesis story is not objective history but is a subjective artistic explanation for an unknown beginning. The verbal artists were inspired to make the beginning subjectively human-like so as to be comprehensible, as objective evidence and science was completely lacking and non-comprehensible.

Monotheism is a simple cognitive strategy to make known an unknown beginning. Monotheistic religion is built on the memory of many forefathers reduced to one by imagining a first father and glorifying it to be a god who made all things of the environment and life.

For monotheistic religions, the beginning of the environment and life is associated with a greater intelligence of a first father god.

As a continuation of the earth environment, the evolved human cerebral cortex imagines and invents both tools and a first father god so as to better survive. A human-like god exists only in the cerebral cortex as an idea and is artistically imagined and adorned with differing names and attributes. A first father god is a purely imaginary way of humans assisting humans to survive the environment and each other.

Human internal conscience is projected outward to an imagined external monotheistic god who observes and assists humans. Human imagination fashions an external observer to be obedient to, a first father ancestor god. The imagined ancestor god serves as an authoritative way of mediating individual and group conduct.

A first father god is a much bigger conceived conscience implanted in the brains of the young and gullible adults. Having children accept the authority of an imaginary first father, is a way of reinforcing the authority of living family fathers. The idea of a first father god is a supplement to parental family authority and it functions to supplement and reinforce a weak individual conscience. The artistically portrayed forefather god also represents social authority of the group and the mutual support of those individuals who accept the artistic imagining of a first father god.

God Maker

The individual often finds it difficult to adjust to internal and external conditions of living. To help solve the problems of existence, the human cerebral cortex of the brain imagines a numerical first father maker of the environment and life.

Monotheistic religion is not a science nor is it a system of mathematics. Human science and reasoning advocate theory, not belief. A theory is an assertion based on observation, material evidence, and language. In contrast, a monotheistic religion is based on artistic imagination, theistic speak and writings, and beliefs and rituals that are emotionally accepted over time into a tradition.

A monotheistic god is an artistic word portrayal of the beginning of the environment and life. Prior to objective science, only a subjective artistic beginning could be imagined and portrayed, not in theory but in verbal and written tribal story.

Monotheistic writings insist that a first father god cannot be portrayed with earthly materials such as stone, metal sculptures, drawings, or paintings. Instead, only words are used to portray a first father god. It is insisted by monotheistic religion that a universal god cannot be seen with the eyes and cannot be directly known by the brain/mind. Therefore, faith is required for what is in reality only a subjective idea and cannot ever be objectively perceived and known. Faith accepts the subjective idea of a god in the brain as a way to pragmatically identify the origin of life and to feel protected.

The monotheistic religions of Judaism, Christianity, and Islam, emphasize an intelligent first father god who dictates rules or commandments to humans as a way to instill social order. To emphasize a first father god is in reality an emphasis on the cerebral cortex of the brain. The worship of a first father god is the subjective worship of the human cerebral cortex. The location of a first father god resides only in the human cerebral cortex of the brain as artistic imagining. The cerebral cortex of the brain is the god maker. In many cultures, the human brain, has imagined and artistically fashioned many gods and goddesses portrayed through images of sculpture, painting, and abstractly with words and scriptures.

A first father god is metaphysical to the extent that it exists only as an abstract idea conceived in the physical cerebral cortex of the brain. A monotheistic god is subjectively revealed as an idea in the cerebral cortex. The idea of a first father is not received from an objective external god.

What a waste of time for the medieval monks of Europe and the Middle East, and theologians, rabbis, priests, ministers, and imams of all time, in a serious tone to blab on about the higher intelligence of a first father god. Observing reality, the higher intelligence is but a projection of the cerebral cortex of the human brain.

Monks often live in deprivation and painful individual denial of basic comforts. Yet they never manage to solve the puzzle of the origin of existence nor of the human soul. Monks stubbornly persist in the blind ignorance of tradition, resulting in stupidity. Stubbornness is a trait that easily progresses into stupidity, and just a small amount of stubbornness over time, can increase into a lot of stupidity known as monotheism. This fact is simultaneously both sad and amusing.

Monotheistic lay persons, monks, and ascetics seek to comprehend a god, soul, and another dimension. Yet the aspirants fail to find a first father god and fail to find a special soul. Only a few may be partially successful in glimpsing another dimension or afterlife. In contrast, a good number of nonreligious individuals have had a spontaneous near-death experience and share the experience of an afterlife dimension in books and lectures. A significant number of unreligious and average young individuals report childhood memories of reincarnation.

Pain Reliever

A monotheistic human-like god is the artistic imagining of a first father beginning. Not sensing the beginning of existence, it is better to subjectively imagine it rather than not having any knowledge of it at all. Therefore, the problem of knowing the origin of existence is solved by imagining and artistically telling a story about a first father beginning.

This is only accomplished by a rudimentary analogical reasoning process in the cerebral cortex of the human brain. What observes and measures and attempts to adjust right and wrong, good and bad, is the cerebral cortex of the brain. This ability of the cerebral cortex is magnified and then attributed to an imagined first father god. A first father god is a traditional ideational pain reliever when the real pain relievers of medications are lacking or ineffective.

The pain reliever of an imagined first father god who made all things new can be appealed to for relief from personal pain by making a better or renewed situation for an individual.

In distress an individual turns to find relief. Finding little or no relief in real experience, an individual may seek to remove himself from the situation by appealing to an imagined first father maker of all situations. The imagined god is appealed to in prayer to make a better situation. Attention is directed to a first father maker when in reality attention should be directed to the supportive earth and the biological ability for reproduction through an evolving sequence of fathers. To revere human origin is realistically to revere the earth and to revere the sexual activity of forefathers and mothers.

Oftentimes, crushing experiences assail an individual life and an imagined super first father brings some subjective pain relief. For those who accept monotheistic religions, imaginary help is better than having no help at all. Appeal to help from earthly fathers is often uncertain and ineffectual but appealing to a first father who cared to make the earth a place for life is a comforting delusion, a mistaken idea.

An individual must be taught or learn how to subjectively accept the idea of an objective first father god who made all things. This ideational comfort exists only in the cerebral cortex of the brain and exclusively for humans. This learned maneuver is the ideational effort to lift an individual out of a situation of burden, struggle, and suffering. Orienting to an unlimited beginning is a way of finding relief from now experience of limited and painful situations. A human-like god is an imaginary accompaniment through life and death.

The practice of monotheism is the learning to accept an imaginary companion on the journey through life in the inevitable direction of death. A first father god is a pain reliever that is only subjectively effective. The metaphor of a human-like first father god breaks down and is ineffective in objective reality. This dismaying truth is seen in the poignant words of Jesus:

"And about the ninth hour Jesus cried with a loud voice, saying, Eli, Eli, lama sabachthani? That is to say, My God, my God, why hast thou forsaken me?" (Matthew 27:46)

The words of Jesus begs a question, did he knowingly use the terms father and god as metaphors, or was he culturally conditioned by tradition to accept the view of an actual first father god? If the latter, then he was disillusioned in the end by his suffering on the cross. Jesus was mistaken in his thinking that the afterlife dimension is made and provided by a first father god.

If pain is not now in an individual life, the person will not have to wait long as it will all too soon arrive. The daily physical and mental pain of many is excessive and overwhelming at times. Some humans may then turn away from an imagined first father god, and instead turn to real drugs, alcohol, food, or relationships that are valued as pain relievers. While sought as relievers of pain, these also serve as inducers of suffering. While a monotheistic first father god is an imaginary pain reliever, death is the real pain reliever of life.

Placebo

Human vulnerability and the struggle to survive the environment and life, cause the Middle Eastern syndrome of imagining a human-like culprit, a first father god who made the hazardous environment and life. This is done so as to reduce human fear and anxiety of the unknown, and to obtain care and protection for the vulnerable individual. The syndrome continues to affect many today with the same symptoms.

A first father god is a placebo, an imaginary idea presented as real and told to the unsuspecting by tradition, monotheistic authorities, fervent converts, and parents to children. Like other placebos, what appears to be real is but a sugar or sweet concoction. Similarly, naïve people in life are given the sugar coated placebo of a first father god.

In nearly every clinical trial that utilizes a placebo, thirty-three percent of participants who receive the placebo, experience the same ameliorative or curative effect as those who receive a real medicine or treatment. In the same way the prayers of some to a first father god are seemingly answered. A god is said to heal a person but what really heals is when the cerebral cortex of the brain has a higher attitude. The idea of a caring and helping first father god is a suggestion that results in placebo healing.

Cultural Differences

The early Greek, Hindu, and Chinese cultures directed attention to observation of the environment and life, and when not overly influenced by superstition, drew some intelligent conclusions of real knowledge. For example, the medicinal treatments of Hippocrates, (circa 460-370 BCE) and Greek philosophy. India developed yoga to relax the body and meditation to cultivate mental and emotional health. The Chinese developed a prodigious knowledge of herbal medicine and many inventions, including paper, ink, paper money, printing, gunpowder, magnetic compass, mechanical clock, tea production, and silk. China also developed the umbrella, acupuncture, iron smelting, porcelain, bronze, kites, rockets, plow, row crop farming, toothbrush, dominoes, and playing cards, just to name a few.

Unlike other cultures of the Middle East, such as the Egyptians and Sumerians, the Semitic Jews observed little of the environment and life, developed few inventions and methods of inquiry, and instead relied on superstition and the rabbinical artistic imaginary storytelling of a first father god.

For early Jewish peoples, there is little observation and discovery. Instead there was a focus of attention on developing a better social order by conceiving of a numerical first father and elevating and exalting it to god status. The internally conceived idea of a first father god is pushed to the outside and spoken of as actually existent and believed to be the cause of phenomena.

This mistake, this originating sin or separation, this cognitive distorting disorder, has become a psychological contagion that continues to infect many to this day and hour.

The separating sin of monotheistic religion is that humans naively imagine a complete goodness of a first father god in a sequence of good and bad biological fathers. Humans also mistake the idea of a first father god to be the result of reliable human reasoning when in reality it is based on artistic imagination, word artistry, traditional belief, and faith.

God and Soul

The real task of ministers, rabbis, and imams, is to encourage individuals to follow the commands of a greater reasoning first father god. In reality, monotheistic functionaries encourage listeners to follow the higher conscious reasoning of the cerebral cortex of the brain, and to moderate the less conscious and subconscious knowing expressions of the triune soul as a forcible hunger for food, sex and reproduction, and aggression.

Attention directed to a monotheistic first father god may be subjectively fulfilling but objectively is a foolish waste of time. A first father god is a subjective and emotionally compelled pure act of creative artistic imagination. A first father god remains ever unseen and never intervenes except as a manipulator of the environment and weather, and to reward and punish humans.

Monotheism imagines and elevates the origin of existence to be a first father and then exalts it to also be a human-like god. Imagining and emphasizing human origin to be a first father god, deemphasizes the internal animating human soul and ignores it to be a continuation of the environment. A focus of attention on a first father god also contributes to ignoring that the human soul is a continuation of a greater cosmological force that furnishes the momentum for the continuous and real relative motion of the universe.

The human soul remains unseen by human eyes. Most are too busy living to search for and to find an essence of life and death. Is there an animating essence of life and is there a human essence that continues after physical death? It is certainly popular to think that something exists within the human body that survives physical death, and yet the concept of a soul varies widely from culture to culture. A human soul is considered by some to be purely imaginary and nonexistent, including the monotheistic religions and of course modern science.

Monotheistic religions continue to not accept the view of an essence of life and death, and maintain the view that only a first father god has the essential essence to animate and reanimate life. When someone dies in the monotheistic tradition, the life is observed to no longer be inside the body. In the three monotheistic religions, the missing life of the body cannot exist on its own and can only be restored by the maker of the body, a first father god. The animating force of life resides and is applied only from outside the human body by a first father originator. Life is placed inside or removed from the body at the sole discretion and whim of a first father god.

For monotheistic religions, humans do not have an immortal or undying substance. What is immortal exists only outside to shape a dependent mortal human body from the soil of the earth. After death, the human body must be reanimated, reformed, remade, and resurrected completely and only from the outside by the first father god. In monotheistic religions, the human body lacks an autonomous animating soul and instead is solely dependent on an artistically imagined first father god.

Image

The best simple image that serves to explain the nonscientific origin of the environment and life is that of a first father god. In the Garden of Eden story, the first father god endowed humans with basic knowledge of work and intellectual tasks of naming things. (Genesis 2:15, 19-20) To work and name things is the ability and task of the conscious reasoning self.

The god also stored some of his own knowledge forbidden to humans in the Tree of Knowledge of Good and Evil. Humans then increased their knowledge by eating the fruit of the tree. An increase of knowledge also brings along with it, a basic inability to know future and full consequences that even good knowledge can bring. Even intended good knowledge is always accompanied by unintended and often bad consequences.

Along with an increase of easily obtained good conscious knowledge from the Tree of Knowledge of Good and Evil, also came some less conscious and subconscious evil knowledge. Evil knowledge obtained from the tree is that of sex and reproduction, along with a consequent curse by the god to inflict a human struggle for food and aggression.

Humans are made in the image of the biblical god (Genesis 1:26-27) who knowing how to make humans with genitals, must also be endowed with them. The first father designed the equipment for sex and reproduction but did not activate the organs or give humans knowledge of them. The forbidden knowledge contained in the fruit of the tree, a symbol for innate knowledge of nature, activated the genitals with which the god endowed his first two humans. Humans then sexually reproduced, obviously an inferior human mode of knowledge and reproduction that brings death.

Utilizing superior knowledge, the god made life utilizing his greater intelligence and the words of his male mouth, a body opening superior to the inferior womb opening of human women. Sexual reproduction is of necessity accompanied by the pain of an accursed toil to care for and protect life by providing food and by necessity to express and defend against aggression.

Sad and Pathetic

Monotheistic religion and its first father god is an artistic way of obtaining relief from not knowing the beginning of existence, and is a way of finding relief from the daily stresses and dangers of life.

The first father is credited with having a perfect intelligence who cares for less intelligent humans. In reality, it is from a very simple human intelligence that a human-like god is fabricated into a crude story of the beginning of existence. The embarrassingly primitive artifice of story serves as a pointer in the direction of what is good in life, its beginning. What has moved the environment into existence and animated life is portrayed to be a first father god. The beginning is an imagined false good that poorly explains the good and evil experiences of life.

Life is a continuation of what is greater but not necessarily good. A first father god is only the human idea of a greater beginning that occurred in a brief seven days. Realistically, life began not with a great first father god but in a greater matrix of time, millions of years ago in the extraordinary matrix of the environment. Life is a continuation of a greater environment, a much greater amount of time, and a greater cosmological force.

Humans continue in the tradition of the imagined first maker by making things from the earth. The effort of making things and also reproducing life is then valorized and sanctioned as worthwhile and not as worthless or futile. Artistically portraying the beginning of existence as good is a human way of making life good, even though life is replete with its numerous evils. But from where have the evils of life come from?

In the biblical Genesis story, humans are portrayed as obtaining their evil knowledge not directly from the good first father but from a storage facility of the god, a special tree. This amusing fictional tale has over the last two thousand years been treated as truth by so many gullible people. Such a sad and pathetic cognitive state of Middle East and Western cultures who accept this fictional and artistic simple story as some kind of profound truth.

Life Coach

Essentially, a monotheistic functionary is an early version of what is today known as a "life coach." Both career individuals lack a depth of knowledge of the body, brain, and behavior history of humankind. Instead, both are naïve and remain superficially ignorant and optimistic toward life. The counsel of both may work for a short time until confidence eventually fades while navigating the bumpy pothole roads of life.

Life coaches want their clients to feel good, do well, and be a better person. Monotheistic functionaries want the same but also rely on an imaginary companion to assist them. Priests, ministers, rabbis, and imams perform as a life coach assisted by an imaginary companion of a first father god. By imagining a first father god and convincing others to accept the subjective idea to be objectively real, religious functionaries work to inspire an individual to live a better life and also to be helpful to others.

The Wall

The Western Wall or Wailing Wall in Jerusalem forms a base support for the Temple Mount upon which the Jewish Temple was located until demolished in 70 CE. Today the Western Wall is a substitute place of worship where oftentimes petitioners can be observed weeping and praying for answers to life's numerous problems, and where some mourn and pray for restoration of the Temple.

The Western Wall is a limestone retaining wall constructed by Herod the Great (74-4 BCE) who built the structure circa 19 BCE. The retaining wall encases a natural steep hill and slope to form a rectangular elevated platform structure known as the Temple Mount. The exposed Western Wall is one hundred ninety feet in length and has an adjoining plaza area. The above ground height of the wall is approximately sixty feet and consists of twenty-eight courses of stone above ground.

The retaining wall was built to support the base for the Temple in which the monotheistic first father god dwelled therein.

However, the Romans destroyed the Temple in the year 70 CE. The god Yhwh obviously did not protect the building and took flight never to return to this very day and hour.

The Islamic al Aqsa mosque built 705 CE sets atop the site previously occupied by the Jewish Temple. Obviously the forefather god ignores his petitioners request for reconstruction of the temple atop the mount, and instead seems to prefer the presence and building of his Islamic descendants over his Jewish progeny.

All monotheists build a supportive and protective wall around themselves by imagining a first father god to assist in the struggles of living. Not with the body but with the cerebral cortex of the brain, the religions of monotheism psychologically build a wall of thoughts that can support and help an individual to endure life by orienting to an imagined first father god.

Buildings

All temples, synagogues, churches, cathedrals, masjids, mosques, and other monotheistic buildings are said to be sacred or holy places in which to gather. Observing reality, the buildings are mundane, built to harbor those entering who accept an artistically imagined first father god. Higher building structures raise attention to what is higher and persuade individuals that what is higher is a first father god located outside of them. In reality, what is worshipped is the cerebral cortex of the brain that imaginatively constructs and accepts a first father god.

What is higher is located inside the cerebral cortex of the brain that seeks to command the lower cerebellum, midbrain, and autonomic nervous system of the body, and the changing environment. The idea of a first father god has been repeatedly built upon and advocated by monotheistic authorities through at least the past twenty centuries.

All buildings of monotheistic religions ostensibly honor the higher objective reality of a first father god.

More truthfully, the buildings are a meeting place that honors the subjective cerebral cortex of the human brain that alone can make higher and better choices and behaviors for humankind. A greater intelligence is attributed to a first father god rather than having the comprehension that it is the cerebral cortex of the brain being worshipped. To assemble in a monotheistic religious service is an individual and group effort to emphasize the cerebral cortex of the brain, an appeal to the higher intelligence of each other, yet projected by the cerebral cortex to be an intelligent and superior first father.

A monotheistic building of worship is a sanctuary and a shrine to what is higher, the beginning of existence that is imagined by the cerebral cortex of the brain to be a first father. In reality, a first father god is imagined by and represents the cerebral cortex of conscious artistic imagining. To enter into a building to worship a monotheistic first father, is to enter into the cerebral cortex of the brain, the only location where the god truly dwells as a subjective idea. The conceived monotheistic god is only located in the higher area of the brain, the cerebral cortex. The buildings of monotheistic worship are a special place for what is higher, and so attendees dress up to wear and look their best, and each behaves on a respectful higher rather than a lower level. This is a higher level of thinking that occurs only in the cerebral cortex of the human brain.

A monotheistic building of worship represents a refuge from all that is lower, the nonconscious environment, and the less conscious cerebellum, midbrain, plexuses, and organs of the human body. A monotheistic building is a sharp demarcation from the land that surrounds it, and forms a distinction between what is sacred and higher, and what is profane and lower. The external sacred building represents the internal higher level human cerebral cortex of the brain, while the profane land surrounding the building represents the lower functions of the human cerebellum, midbrain, and body.

Entering into a religious building to join and observe others in the worship of a monotheistic god, is a poor, shallow, and lazy social way to comprehend the beginning of existence. The better way to comprehend is to enter into the temple of the body to observe conscious and subconscious brain and body functions.

To know the origin of life there has to be close observation of the environment, and individual human brain and body functions. Then can be better observed, comprehended, and confirmed that the soul is a triune forcible hunger for food, sex and reproduction, and aggression. The triune soul can be observed and confirmed to be a continuation of energy elements of the earth, and the environment to be a continuation of a cosmological force that moves the universe.

Favor

Jews favor commandments bestowed by the first father god Yhwh to socially control individual behaviors. Muslims favor submitting their behaviors five times daily to the first father god Allah. Christians favor the commandments of Jesus to love a metaphorical first father god and nearby neighbors as one's self. The first father god of these monotheistic religions is a bare orientation, a subjective metaphor that serves to only mildly influence conscious and subconscious human behaviors.

A monotheistic god is a subjective metaphor utilized to counter and direct a real animating triune soul to what is good. Imagining a first father god only superficially solves the problem of the individual soul, the less conscious and subconscious forcible behaviors for food, sex and reproduction, and aggression.

The doctrine of Original Sin is advocated by the Christian theologian St Augustine (354-430 CE). This official doctrine of the Catholic church is a mere myth to explain the real human triune soul as a forcible hunger for food, sex and reproduction, and aggression. The lower knowledge of the midbrain and body, offends and conflicts with the higher intelligence of the cerebral cortex of the brain, portrayed in Christian mythic doctrine as a first father god.

The biblical first father god made his people without an animating soul. The Jewish religion and that of its sects of Christianity and Islam, are therefore entirely dependent on their subjective belief of a forefather god that will someday remake and resurrect the body.

In contrast, the Hindu culture developed and favors the praiseworthy methods of yoga and meditation to better explore the conscious and subconscious brain and body functions. In India, a real animating soul or atma is recognized and acknowledged to be a problem most worthy of solving. From ancient India, ever continues to flow forth a clear stream of wisdom that refreshes and awakens an individual to the wonder and challenge of self and soul exploration. Salutations to the wise of India! Only India of all the lands of the earth has shown the way to the wisdom of all time.

Failure

Monotheists worship the beginning of the environment and life to be a universal first father god. Out of an abundance of ignorance, monotheists fail to notice how the human cerebral cortex imagines and artistically shapes with words the subjective idea of a first father god. Humans fail to notice their true origin to be a triune soul as a forcible hunger for food, sex and reproduction, and aggression. Humans also fail to trace the soul to the energy elements of the environment and these to a cosmological force that moves all things into, through and out of existence.

The human cerebral cortex is capable of conscious reasoning (Latin ratio, measure) as it measures external objects in space and time images. The cerebral cortex also makes a measured or reasoned response of behavior and adjusts to hunger for food, sex and reproduction, and aggression.

The conscious reasoning self finds it difficult to adjust and to control the subconscious nonreasoning soul, one's own and that of others. The reasoning cerebral cortex of the brain is easily overwhelmed by the nonreasoning midbrain and body dynamic of the soul.

The reasoning and image making cerebral cortex of the brain seeks to solve the difficulties of living, the external environment and the internal animating soul.

What good does it really do to study human history and remnant cultural artifacts, and to ignore and not investigate the animating force of behaviors? The animating force of life is the triune soul of hunger for food, sex and reproduction, and aggression. This dynamic is a continuation of the supportive elements of energy of the earth, and is a continuation of the relative forms and motion of the environment, all a continuation of a cosmological force.

Best

A monotheistic first father god has the best intelligence, love, and strength that humans can imagine. Humans have to think that the god must have the best intelligence to make so many complicated things of the earth and life, and must also be very strong to make the environment. Humans have a very low level intelligence, love, and strength. Therefore, humans can only imagine a first father and then artistically embellish the notion of a god having greater qualities and foolishly accept their own subjective imaginations to be reliable and true knowledge.

It cannot be said the best attributes and qualities of intelligence, love, and strength belong to the human soul. Middle East religions of Judaism, Christianity, and Islam, do not accept that humans have an animating soul. For these religions, humans only have the life of the body made from the soil of the earth that the first father god must one future day resurrect from the dead.

Search

The early Jews searched for good in the environment, among fellow humans, and within the individual body and brain. They surely experienced much disappointment.

Some relative good and pleasures are found in the environment and within fellow humans, and yet these are always accompanied by evils and pain. Little real and enduring good is found upon the earth, so Jewish attention instead turned to imagining the good of a first father beginning of the environment, life, and humans.

Orientation to the past and a first father beginning continues to attract many. Fervent monotheists will never easily accept the comprehension that will take away a human-like beginning and future ending, nor that of now moments of protection furnished by a first father god.

There can only be imagined a good beginning such as the Garden of Eden story when hunger for food, sex and reproduction, and aggression did not exist. This artistic imagined story of Genesis is a retreat to an imagined past good, and is a psychological longing and way of lifting an individual out of an inexorable cause and effect sequence of good and evil life experience,.

The good of a protective god is also projected into the future to remake the body during a resurrection. Monotheistic religions have a last or final judgement when a good first father god will ironically inflict both the good of reward and the evil of punishment upon humans. The imagining of a monotheistic good first father god who made the good and evil earth, and who will one fine future day make the earth a good place to live, and will reanimate the one and only body, and reward and punish, is a real and continuing delusion of the cerebral cortex of the human brain.

Rumor

The word rumor is defined as:

"Unverified information usually spread by word of mouth; a story in general circulation lacking confirmation, certainty, or facts. News or story passed from person to person that may or may not be true; gossip, hearsay."

Writings or scriptures that mention a first father god are but religious rumors, social gossip of unverified stories that do not exist in fact, and are mere imaginative artistic expressions of the beginning of existence. When a person is converted to a monotheistic point of view of a first father god, they are accepting a simplistic story as a way of identifying the beginning of existence and as a way to establish patriarchal authority and social order.

The forceful earth environment is great in size. Looking at the seeming rising and setting sun on the horizon, there is sensed by the human eye and brain, a greater unknown force that moves the earth and sun, the moon, distant stars, and galaxies. The appearance and disappearance of the sun on the horizon also suggests to human ken, another and possible better unobserved dimension of reality. This ken is marred by imagining there to be a greater kin of a monotheistic first father god.

Precarious

The English word precarious is defined as:

"Lacking ease or assurance, dangerously lacking stability or security; subject to chance or unknown conditions and circumstances that tip one way and then another; dependent on another or on conditions and situations beyond personal control."

Conceiving of a first father maker, and exalting it to be a god, is the way the cerebral cortex of the brain seeks help during precarious life experiences. A monotheistic god is the way humans help themselves by artistically imagining a first father in a genealogical line of human fathers.

If little care is the reality between fellow humans, predator animals, and the environment, then some relief is obtained by artistically imagining a caring first father who is exalted to the status of a god. Each individual needs real help yet it only exists as an ersatz relief of an imagined first father maker and helper god.

Brain

Monotheism is a big payday. Many members donate offerings to their favored monotheistic religion and to its leaders. Many bequeath money in their wills to the religions. For providing an explanation of the beginning, for providing imaginary care and protection, and for inspiring others with hope that often turns out to be false, monotheistic sacerdotalists collect a big payday. Realistically, a human-like first father god is a conceived concept, an artistic imagining of the cerebral cortex of the human brain.

The biblical intelligent father god of Genesis, is portrayed as condemning and punishing the first two humans. This is a mythic storied way of portraying the conscious cerebral cortex of the brain and central nervous system to be in conflict with the subconscious cerebellum, midbrain, and autonomic nervous system of the body. The imagined god represents the real intelligent human cerebral cortex. The behavioral disobedience of the first two humans represents the subconscious dynamic of the triune soul, as a forcible hunger for food, sex and reproduction, and aggression. A human-like god is the ideational daily attempt by the cerebral cortex of the brain to refrain from the dynamic of the cerebellum, midbrain, and autonomic nervous system of the body, the dynamic of which is the animating soul.

A first father god story is a mechanism that portrays the human attempt to stay in the vicinity of the good of higher reasoning and rules of behavior as conceived by the cerebral cortex of the brain. The imagined good of a first father god is the individual and social attempt to reduce the harm from the external environment, and from the harm wrought by the internal triune soul of hunger for food, sex and reproduction, and aggression.

The generating of a first father god in the cerebral cortex of the brain is an imaginative and primitive way of explaining the distant past of human generations. The imagining and accepting of a first father god is a personal and social attempt to have the cerebral cortex of the brain command and rule the individual and society.

The cerebral cortex can make better interpersonal ethical choices and can promote social cohesion and cooperation.

A first father god is a contrived human attempt to reinforce the conscious cerebral cortex and to thereby rule the nonconscious environment and the less conscious of animal life. The utilization of a first father god is an attempt to overrule the less conscious midbrain and body functions. These are the domain of the dynamic triune soul. The good of reasoning by the cerebral cortex is sought as the way to transcend the harmful individual essence of life; the unreasoning triune soul of hunger, sex, and aggression.

The rule of a first father is in reality the rule of the cerebral cortex of the brain where the artistic imagining of a god takes place. A first father god is a way of identifying and locating a beginning and what is good. The cerebral cortex of the human brain can think of good things with which to improve life such as tools, weapons, shelters, conveyances, and including an imagined human-like beginning of care, a first father god. A first father god is a psychological attempt to put aside and to reduce the individual human capacity to inflict harm, violence and evil.

Humans make things. Humans also utilize analogy to extrapolate that life and all the large complicated things and functions of the environment, must have been made by a superior intelligence, a first father god. What the analogy asserts in reality is that the primacy of the conscious cerebral cortex of the human brain must prevail over the nonconscious environment, less conscious other living species, and the less conscious and subconscious cerebellum, midbrain, and autonomic nervous system of the human body.

The conscious imagined good of a god, is secondary to and supported by a primary individual subconscious interest of survival. The continuing monotheistic emphasis on the good of a god is the psychological effort and attempt to go where good is, to be with the good, and receive what is good, and its converse to reduce, avoid, and escape what is not good, the harm of daily living.

A first father god is a socially accepted and imaginary way of protecting an individual from the deception, disappointments, and emotional and physical harm of life and death.

Beginning

Knowledge of the beginning of humans is manufactured by the human brain to be human-like. A first father god is therefore an artistic product of the brain. In the past, few other theories of the beginning of the environment and life existed. The emphasis on a monotheistic god is in reality an over valuing of the cerebral cortex of the brain that imagines and projects its origin to be a first father.

A universe with an imagined invisible first father background is intended to make existence friendlier. Yet based upon what humans experience daily, if the origin of life was a first father, it would have to be not a friendly parent-like god but more like an unfriendly enemy.

Identify

Whatever has brought life into existence is neither good nor human-like. The triune soul in cells as a forcible hunger for food, sex and reproduction, and aggression did not get there by what is human-like or intelligent. The motion and function of cells is a continuation of energy and force. A first father god is a primitive human way of identifying the unseen force that moves the universe, and from which the environment and life have come into existence. Yet there is no first father god that forces the universe to be in perpetual motion, or that forces life to live.

The momentum of the visible universe is attributed by a sizable portion of the earth's population to a first father god beginning. In reality, the relative motion and momentum of existence is ongoing as a continuation of a cosmological force that ever exists on its own.

There is a cosmological force that forces the universe to move as energy elements and as material forms of asteroids, comets, stars, moons, and planets. Forceful elements of energy of the earth continue in living forms as a triune soul of forcible hunger for food, sex and reproduction, and aggression.

The irrational soul function of life is the origin of and supports the evolved borderline rational cerebral cortex of the human brain. Middle Eastern cultures have utilized the artistic ability of the cerebral cortex for words and story to imagine a first father god as a way to identify the beginning of the environment and life.

With the accepted presence of a first father god, humans are also prompted to think and act on a higher level. A good first father god is a simplistic way for the cerebral cortex to identify and find a higher good. To be more god-like is to emphasize the capacity of the cerebral cortex of the human brain. Following the commandments of a human-like god, is in reality to follow the higher knowledge of the cerebral cortex. Higher knowledge is followed rather than the lesser and lower knowledge of the essence of life, the triune soul as a forcible hunger for food, sex and reproduction, and aggression. To know more is the real extent of reaching for what is higher, imagined to be a first father god.

All of the religious hymns ever written and sung in praise of a monotheistic god, in reality extoll the cerebral cortex of the brain that has the higher knowledge to artistically imagine a human-like beginning of a first father god A first father god is an artistic makeshift solution to know a beginning of existence and life, and to secure protection in an insecure environment.

The conscious cerebral cortex also feigns superiority over the animating life force and subconscious growth and function of the body. This is the triune soul as a forcible hunger for food, sex and reproduction, and aggression.

Comfort

A conceived first father god is the imaginary attempt to bring about ethical, moral, and social order and cooperation among members of a society. A first father god is an imaginary mechanism for the instilling of order in the daily disorder of individual and social life. Monotheistic religions seek to override a harmful environment and the harmful behavior of humans by appealing to an imagined first father god of care. The idea of a first father god is an imagined comfort utilized to soften the real harshness of living and dying.

Christian children are taught comforting prayers to a first father god. A prayer taught to children by parents reveals the adult need for care and protection during the vulnerable state of subconscious sleep.

"Now I lay me down to sleep,
I pray the lord my soul to keep.
If I should die before I wake,
I pray the lord my soul to take."

A first father is subjectively conceived and then objectified, placed external to humans as an object. What is conceived is then believed to exist objectively. The unbiblical but popular folk prayer also mentions the living body to have a soul that survives physical death.

Savior

No god exists in reality to save the human soul. In reality, the soul saves the individual, yet the soul has been ignored and downgraded by monotheistic religions to instead favor a first father god. The soul saves an individual by default, by being a continuation of the energy of the earth and a continuation of a non-decaying cosmological force that ever exists on its own.

The essence of human life is rumored to be good and therefore worthy of saving. Humans may consciously sense a vague subconscious animating force inside of the body. Yet the soul of bodily life is not perceived as distinct and is instead confounded with the cerebral cortex function of the brain.

The soul is less of a conscious intelligence and is much more a non-cerebral lesser and subconscious intelligence of the cerebellum, midbrain, and body as animated by a triune force. That which moves the universe also forcibly moves life to hunger for food, moves life to behaviors of sex and reproduction, and to aggression.

Material forms of the environment corrode and erode and are pulverized to return to a finer energy origin. In contrast, life encounters accident, aggression, disease, ageing, and physical death. Life is akin to the material environment and also follows the behavior pattern of wearing away and reverts to an energy formation. The energy elements of material forms tend to randomize.

As a continuation of a cosmological force and earth energy, the forcible essence of the animating triune soul as hunger for food, sex and reproduction, and aggression, may tend to cohere as a pattern and to continue to exist extra-dimensionally. Recent medical and psychological case studies of near-death experience and many past and present anecdotal reports of survival lend support and some credence to this assertion.

Twenty-First Century Worship

Sometime during the twenty-first century, the cerebral cortex of the brain must and will be recognized and worshiped as the imaginative artistic maker of any and all human-like gods. An image of the awe inspiring cerebral cortex should be installed prominently in temples of worship. Along with it, the more awe inspiring triune soul can be displayed by the cerebellum, midbrain, and body, and abstractly by the twenty-third letter of the Greek alphabet known as psi Ψ, often utilized as the symbol for psyche.

The tines of the trident should be labeled as hunger, sex and reproduction, and aggression. The two side tines of the trident are joined by a longer extended center. The longer center should be recognized as a symbol for the continuation of an unseen sole cosmological force that should be worshiped as the impetus of all relative motion of the environment and life.

Cosmological force can also be symbolically represented by a changing mobile of the moving cosmos. These should rightfully be the accoutrement of worship and true religion in the twenty-first century and beyond.

Metaphor

A first father god is a metaphorical greater good that transcends the lesser relative goods and the many evils of human life experience. The conception of a beginning as human-like occurs as rudimentary analogical reasoning. For monotheism, humans had to have first come from what is human-like, from a first father ancestor magnified in imagination to be a god and all good. This erroneous and impaired simple imagining is false and yet is comforting to many through the multitude discomforts of living.

The mythic Garden of Eden story portrays the struggle of human life to be a result of acquiring good and evil knowledge not directly from the god but from a fruit tree. The first father god is portrayed as cursing human life he had made. In reality, all of life is a continuation of the supportive earth. The mythic Garden of Eden tale is a sin, an imaginary story separation from a real origin of life as a continuation of the earth and solar environment.

By artistically imagining a first father beginning, the fictional story separates humans from a true earthly origin. For monotheistic religions, metaphysics consists of a childishly appealing artistic story of an imaginary first father god. The monotheistic and artistic imaginary beginning wrought by a first father god, continues to delude many, and provides an often disappointing yet not uncomfortable delusion.

Lacking knowledge of where humans came from in the past, the biblical writer(s) of Genesis imagined a metaphorical beginning of a first father god. The authors artistically fashioned a simple story of how the environment and human life came into existence.

The imagined first father god portrays good knowledge, the real evolved conscious cerebral cortex of the human brain and the central nervous system. The Tree of Knowledge of Good and Evil portrays the knowing function of the subconscious cerebellum, midbrain, and autonomic nervous system of the body. The less conscious or subconscious knowledge is the dynamic of the triune soul. Higher secondary conscious knowledge disapproves of excess obsession with the primary and lower subconscious knowledge of the triune soul as hunger for food, sex and reproduction, and aggression.

Former

The former of life as a verb and noun is that which comes before. No first father god has ever formed life to live. That which has come before, as the former of life, is the earth that nurtures and supports the living. The former of earth are elements of energy as atoms, electrons, and quantum particles. The former of energy is a cosmological force that ever exists on its own.

The animating former of life is a forcible hunger for food, sex and reproduction, and aggression. The former of human life is not a first father god but a genealogical line of forefathers and mothers, and other living forms as nourishment. To imagine a first father as the beginning of a biological line of fathers is a perversion of perception by accepting imagination and a conception to be real. A former first father exists only in imagination and storytelling as a subjective and artistic way of identifying the beginning of existence.

A fantastic first father only exists subjectively in the cerebral cortex of the brain, and a human-like beginning has never occurred. Only a relative long evolved beginning exists from the nearest relative, the earth, as the related real origin of life.

A first father god is a way of making human life special. A fantastic former first father is an inflated faintly lit bubble surround that eerily casts a surrealist and existential gloom over the dim goings on of human daily life.

A monotheistic god is a bubble blown up by human imagination and artistic words of story to surround simplistic thinking humans.

When the first father god of Genesis made the environment and life he pronounced it to be good and even very good. (Genesis 1:10, 12, 18, 21, 25, 31) Yet this pronouncement of good is a fiction of human imagination. In reality, the beginning of life is the good and evil of the environment, and a first father god is an imaginary way of transcending the real good and evil of the environment and life. A real existence always consists of both good and bad, treasures and trash.

Godly

Monotheistic religious leaders encourage followers to obey the commands of a first father god. In reality, the task of a minister, priest, rabbi, or imam, is to coax an individual to follow the higher reasoning of his or her cerebral cortex rather than the lower triune soul as a forcible hunger for food, sex and reproduction, and aggression.

The imagined authority of a good first father god is the ostensible raison d'etre for doing what is good. It is the real destruction resistant soul that is usually out of control and bad. Therefore, a first father god is imagined by the cerebral cortex to control humans by dictating commandments for them to follow.

Godly people are those who aspire to and who rely on an objective first father god. In reality, monotheists rely only on the conscious cerebral cortex of the brain and its ability for subjective artistic imagination. The conceiving of a human-like nonvisible god, is a non-observational and abstract way of identifying the origin of the environment and life. A first father god originates only in artistic imagination of the cerebral cortex and is a referent to human conscious brain function.

A biblical first father god is an artistic way of explaining the beginning sequence of the first environment, life forms, humans, and is a way of explaining the early acquisition of knowledge. The god of the Genesis story endowed the first humans with a basic level of knowledge. The god also surreptitiously stored some of his own special knowledge in a tree, the Tree of Knowledge of Good and Evil. So much for the modern blind notion of an all good god. Humans could not be portrayed as obtaining their evil knowledge directly from the god as this would be a damming indictment of him. The problematic explanation of bad or evil human behavior is deflected to the mechanism of a fruit tree.

A first father god is an imagined nonsexual actor of a beginning that occurred prior to human sexual reproduction. The god does not indulge in sex and is not openly associated with sex, yet he made his first humans in his image. (Genesis 1:27) The male god who made humans in his image, and made them with dormant genitals, did not bestow his troublesome knowledge of sex directly to the first humans. The first humans are portrayed as acquiring it for themselves.

Observing reality, humans acquire knowledge of sex not from a first father god but directly from the innate soul, a dynamic triune forcible hunger for food, sex and reproduction, and aggression. The subconscious body function of growth developmentally reveals the biological knowledge of puberty to conscious knowledge of the cerebral cortex of the brain. The literary artists of Genesis could have better spent their time observing the reality of subconscious body functions rather than relying on conscious imagination and story.

Those who espouse the objective existence of a first father god are simplistic cognitive cripples. The Semitic penchant for artistic imagination and story is a long way from the observational reality of Aryan Hindu yoga practice and Buddhist meditative observation as proven methods of experiential investigation of what exists.

Middle East Semitic artistic imagination and ability for storytelling are no match for the Eastern Aryan observational meditation disciplines utilized to investigate the human conscious self and the subconscious soul.

Seclusion

Siddhartha Gautama, also known as Buddha (circa 623-543 BCE) is accepted by tradition to have commented, "Having seen the glittering golden bracelets well-crafted by the goldsmith clashing against each other on the forearm, let one live solitary like the one-horn rhinoceros." (Sutta Nipata)

Some humans seek seclusion and solitude as a refuge from the disappointments, conflict, and pain of life including human interaction. For some, social deprivation and loneliness is the lesser pain of living. Some few seek privacy and withdraw from or at least reduce the distractions of life so as to better observe, study, and comprehend the environment and brain and body reality functions. It is a luxury and a noble tradition to spend time observing the body and brain with the intention to better comprehend them.

Relatively few withdraw from society for reasons of religion, to seek for and experience a beginning that humans are connected to. The beginning of the environment and life has long been rumored by monotheistic religions to be a first father god. Many accept this monotheistic artistic conception of where all things come from to be satisfactory.

Humans who search for a first father god are seeking for what exists only in human artistic imagination. Those who seek to comprehend a first father god, experience only superficial prayerful ideas and perhaps mild paroxysms of emotion. There will always be a failure to find a real god as there is a failure to observe where the god is truly located. The cerebral cortex of the brain inclines to imagination and artistic creativity as an effort to display and make known the beginning of existence.

When it comes to discussion of the existence of a first father god, authorities and lay people alike mistakenly think they are utilizing reason when in reality they are only relying on artistic imagination, blind faith, and belief of tradition. For the majority seekers of the origin of existence, memory and superficial tradition sidetrack and impair individual comprehension. Monotheists seek to eke out some goodness of existence and for them goodness is conceived to be located in the beginning as a first father god. The god is also imagined to oversee life and to welcome the deceased at the ending of human life.

Animals are not deemed worthy to be so honored. A first father god exists to command only humans, not any other species on the earth. All other species are free to act as they see fit with no interference from the fatherly god.

Roots

Artifact evidence suggests that as long ago as five thousand years, Hindu ascetics of India practiced yoga and also began a tradition of going to the forest in an attempt to find the immortal animating soul of life. While many of them failed in the attempt, some, probably unknown, and at least one known individual succeeded. One Hindu son known as Buddha went to the forest to search for the essence of life, found it, and then taught a discipline to cool and extinguish the animating destruction resistant soul.

Through meditation and comprehension, the animating force of growth inside the body and brain was reduced to a relative calm of nirvana. This is a true emphasis on what the soul is, a force that resists destruction and that animates or reincarnates an individual again and again until successfully reduced.

The adherents of monotheistic religions in the West want to hear about miracles of a first father god or the son of a god, or parental first father ethical commandments to instill individual, ritual, and social order.

There is nearly zero mention in monotheistic scriptures of dynamic methods or techniques to comprehend the human condition. As a result, in Middle East and Western cultures, there is only an excess of popular babbling belief about a first father god.

Words attributed to Siddhartha Gautama or Buddha, (circa 623-543 BCE) utilize a metaphor that refers to "pulling up the roots" of creeper vines and trees. Not to do so leads to regrowth of the vegetation if the roots are not destroyed. Use of this plant model coveys the analogy well that the roots of life come from and are supported, not by a first father god but by the earth.

Like a plant, all of life is rooted in and is supported by the earth. The roots referred to are conscious and subconscious tanha or cravings. Though unmentioned, by this is meant the triune soul, the forcible hunger for food, sex and reproduction, and aggression.

The verses of the Dhammapada are a collection of sayings accepted by tradition to be the spoken words of Buddha. Some of the verses from Chapter 24 are based on observation of plant and tree growth as a metaphor of the soul.

"Whoever is overcome by this wretched craving, his sorrows grow like grass after the rains."

The phrase "wretched craving" is a simile and a synonym for the triune soul, of hunger for food, sex and reproduction, and aggression. There is also a seeking of secondary pleasures of many kinds, including wealth and relief from the pains of living by addictions of alcohol and drugs.

"This I say to you, good success to all assembled here. Dig up the root of craving, like one in search of the fragrant root of the birana grass."

"Not observing, craving increases and grows rampant like a creeper vine."

"Everywhere...the creeper vine sprouts and grows. Seeing that the creeper has sprung up, cut off its root with wisdom."

"Just as a tree, though cut down, sprouts and grows again if its roots remain uncut and vigorous, so too, until craving that lies dormant is rooted out, suffering grows again and again."

For most plants and trees, future root growth exists dormant in the seeds that sprout and grow dependent on suitable conditions. The greater parts of plants and trees are the subterranean roots that are usually two to three time larger in mass than are visible stem, trunk, branches, and leaves.

The conscious human self is like the visible part of plants. The conscious self has its roots in the subconscious subterranean soul. For humans, the hidden roots of life extend to and are a continuation of an animating soul. The soul extends to and is a continuation of the nonconscious environment that is a continuation of a non-appearing cosmological force that ever exists on its own.

The animating essence of life is a forcible growth of hunger for food, sex and reproduction, and aggression. All microorganisms, aerial, aquatic, and terrestrial animals, like plants have their life essence rooted in the earth. The plant analogy of root growth used by Buddha is applied to mean a growing recurrent hunger for food, sex and reproduction, and aggression.

What is the root of craving? For humans craving is rooted in subject-object internal sensations of external objects. These subjective sensations sprout into picture images in the cerebral cortex of the brain, predominantly images of food, sex or its reproductive results, and aggression. Unless observed and disciplined, these images grow rampantly into the willing growth of conscious and subconscious behaviors and habits.

Removing only the visible stem or trunk of a plant or tree, the nonvisible roots will sprout to grow again.

The individual has to go beneath the surface through introspective meditation, observation, and discipline to prune and aspire to extirpate the growing roots. The individual must observe the repetitive craving or willing for, and direct excessive attention away from an object. In this way there is an awakening to and a calming of a destruction resistant animating soul.

The conscious self must tread lightly into the subconscious domain of the soul. It requires conscious effort to turn the animating essence of life, the forcible triune soul, from what it wants as it is a continuation of earth energy and a cosmological force. The conscious self struggles and experiences discomfort and pain in its efforts to subdue or direct the subconscious soul. Sensations and picture images of the conscious self continuously distract a focus of attention. Yet with consistent practice of meditation over time, the ability is acquired to focus attention and to patiently tease apart and tame the forcible triune soul.

No easy task is it for the conscious self to observe and to discipline the subconscious soul. The rush of life, of family and work, occupy most of daily conscious attention. It is good to have a spouse as company but with the relationship comes one thousand and one disagreements and disappointments. Social life is mainly shallow and consists of superficial conversation, generally about acquiring various pleasures and possessions. This lifestyle leaves precious little time for self exploration, and to explore the forcible triune soul that animates life.

Pulling Roots

During daily meditative observation and study, an individual can pull up the roots, the forcible growth of the animating triune soul. The meditator pulls out the roots, the forcible growth of picture images and animating behaviors of eating food, sex and reproduction, and aggression.

The forcible growth of life is the animating essence of a triune soul. During meditation, with consistent practice, an individual can consciously pull out the subterranean subconscious roots. The roots can be pulled up by meditatively observing the forcible growth of sensations of the body, brain picture images, and willing body behaviors. The roots of the forcible growth of hunger for food, sex and reproduction, and aggression can be pulled out by reducing sensations and brain images of them. Through meditative observation the forcible growth of the triune soul is interfered with and is not allowed to overly take root and to forcibly grow. The roots of the soul are pulled up by reducing sensations and by seeing the impermanence of sensations, seeing the impermanence of picture images and impermanence of willing for the pictured objects.

Sensations and picture images are reduced, moderated, redirected, and when possible eliminated. They are not overly suppressed or expressed. Sensations take root to grow into picture images of objects and willing for them. These together are a dynamic, a karmic cluster that rolls along through time. These together, of conscious and subconscious character traits, exist and endure and repeat both here and hereafter.

What is a root made of inside of humans and where is it located? The roots of craving consist of sensations, conscious images and accompanying emotions. The picture images are either memory of the past, or of an imagined future. Feelings and emotions are immediate responses of pain or pleasure that accompany the picture images. The roots are both conscious and subconscious. The self is conscious while the soul is a subconscious forcible hunger for food, sex and reproduction, and aggression.

The subconscious cerebellum, midbrain, and autonomic nervous system have evolved and differentiated the conscious self of the cerebral cortex and central nervous system. Conscious attention struggles with the subconscious soul attention directed by hunger for food, sex and reproduction, and aggression. Wisdom is to see how sensations give rise to picture images in the brain, and how willing behavior for or against the objects then ensues.

A meditative individual pulls out the roots by not indulging in sensations, or by having conscious attention inundated by picture images of past and future to grow in the brain. With a focus of meditative attention he observes the impermanence of sensations, and picture images of past and future, and willing behavior. He does not allow images of past or future to sprout and grow.

From the sexual pleasure of parents, each individual enters onto this landed earth, a place of continuing struggle of both wanting to have or wanting not to have. Life is a forcible struggle of hunger for food, sex and reproduction, and aggression; the animating triune essence of life. The forcible internal struggle of brain and body leads to forcible external struggle of behaviors in the environment. The forcible subconscious body and midbrain, sensations, and conscious brain images lead to behaviors.

The roots of a plant aggressively seek nourishment and water, compete for growing area, and either the roots or tops of plants sexually or asexually reproduce. This subconscious animating process is the triune soul of forcible hunger for food, sex and reproduction, and aggression, and is what animates all of life and enables it to survive.

Though difficult to do, it is quite sane to direct attention and to meditate by observing and exploring mental and physical functions, and to search out an animating soul. It is quite insane to accept without good evidence, a story format of a grand and great first father faux beginning said to be a god.

Meditation explores brain and body functions and explores what forcibly animates life within. The nucleus of life within the body is a continuation of a supportive earth, and not a first father god. The triune soul of a forcible hunger for food, sex and reproduction, and aggression is a continuation of the forcible elements of energy that form the earth, solids, liquid water, gases of the air, and ambient temperature of the sun.

The roots of life can be traced to the environment and to a greater cosmological force of which life is a continuation. Observing the motion of the universe, there can be inferred to exist a greater cosmological force. The local environment has its roots in a nonlocal cosmological force that moves the universe. The triune soul of forcible hunger for food, sex and reproduction, and aggression has its roots in the forcible energy of the element environment. All of life has its roots in the forcible environment of energy elements, forcibly rooted in an unseen cosmological force that moves the universe, and ever exists on its own.

Effort

Meditation calms the conscious effort of the body and the picture images of the brain. Calming conscious muscular efforts of the body, attention can be directed to sensate conscious experience of body parts. Then awareness of subconscious efforts and functions of the body may be reflected in conscious awareness. The conscious and subconscious efforts of hunger for food, sex and reproduction, and aggression, is the effort of the triune soul to exist and to survive.

All conscious and subconscious human effort to live is a continuation of the effort of the universe to move and to exist, namely, a cosmological force that ever exists on its own. This existing on its own, is what the philosopher Immanuel Kant (1724-1804) refers to as the "thing in itself" (German, ding an sich). Yet the term thing in "itself" smacks of anthropomorphism. A cosmological force has no human-like self, it only exists on its own sans a substratum.

Continuing human effort is expended as change by the conscious and subconscious brain and body. Conscious sensations, picture images, and self willing and body behavior for or against is constantly changing and impermanent. Subconscious soul willing and body behavior is constantly changing and impermanent. For humans, conscious self choices and efforts attempt to get pragmatic or better results.

Yet life is lived predominantly by the less conscious and subconscious essential changing efforts of hunger for food, sex and reproduction, and aggression.

Apparent Reality

Humans have in the past, and many continue to accept the view that the sun rises on the horizon of the earth, moves across the sky, and sets to make a day and night. Yet this is only an apparent reality. The sun is stationary relative to the earth in space as it revolves around the Milky Way galaxy. Real motion occurs while the observer stands on the earth that rotates toward or away from the stationary sun. The motion attributed to the sun across the sky, actually occurs as the rotation of the earth on which the observer stands.

In a somewhat similar way, humans mistakenly imagine the impetus for the momentum and motion of the environment and life to be an originating first father god. This occurs as the motion of life is not traced to the environment, and elements of the earth cannot be easily traced to an unapparent cosmological force that continually moves the universe. Instead, by necessity of cognitive limitation, there is imagined to be a parent figure of a first father god.

The daily rotation of the earth produces the visual illusion and delusion of a rising and setting sun. Similarly, during waking life, a first father is ideationally and delusionally hoisted into the heavens above to shine invisibly as an explanation for the beginning of existence and to provide care and protection for humans.

The relative and dependent movement of life is not observed to be a continuation of the motion of the earth. Humans fail to connect the internal movement of life with the energy elements of the environment, and to the external motion of the earth as it rotates on its axis to bring day as it turns toward the sun, and night as it turns away from it.

For theistic religions, the movement of the energy of the elements has not been observed to be an impetus of life.

Instead, an impaired and stubborn cultural tradition of a first father parent god persists as an embedded cultural concept.

Cosmological Continuation

In ancient India, by disciplining attention through the practice of meditation, the conscious self came to recognize the soul or atma as the animating force of life. Life in general was recognized to be animated by the soul within. The result of this aesthetic sensate intuition and conception, is the ethical Hindu teaching of ahimsa or non-harming.

In the more primitive Middle East cultures and religions, there is a cognitive failure to perceive an interior animating force of a soul. Instead of a focus of attention on an animating soul within the body, attention is directed to an animating first father who will remake or resurrect the soulless physical body. The delusion of a generational first father god is imagined to exist exterior to life and the environment by a few, ridiculously accepted over time by many, and spread to and indulged in to its discredit, by a degenerate western culture.

Regressing back over the generational line of forefathers, the intelligent cerebral cortex of monotheists unintelligently fashions a greater intelligent god. The imagined intelligent god is the cerebral cortex that projects its own greater potential and in so doing serves to solve the mystery of an unknown origin. The projected and externalized god also directs human attention to what is an objective good, and away from the excess evils of the environment and living.

Thinking about a first father god is a way of directing and organizing one's thoughts to what is good and of feeling good about being in the vicinity of what is good. A first generation almighty father is needed for hourly and daily protection and care, and for imposing ethical obedience to those living beneath the gaze of the supernatural parent figure.

For monotheists, the only refuge from the frightening and harmful experiences of life is a psychological regression to the time of a beginning and a first father of all later biological fathers.

The cerebral cortex of the brain magnifies human intelligence and exaggerates and imagines it to be a forefather god, the causal maker of the environment and life. In reality, it is the cerebral cortex of the brain that is the artistic maker of a beginning, an expose in scriptural story as a scripted play of imagination.

Humans recoil from the uncaring environment that treats all species of life as throwaways. Some humans respond by seeking refuge and relief by imagining a first father god. Yet, the mechanism of a human-like god is imaginary subjective knowledge that is not objectively true. Life is a continuation of the environment. By imagining a first father god, humans seek to be saved by intentional caring goodness and not to be destroyed by the vicissitudes of nature.

No first father god is located outside of the human cerebral cortex. Humans cannot be saved by an imaginary god but are saved precisely since they are a continuation of the environment composed of energy. The environment of forms is composed of energy of atoms, electrons, and subatomic particles that are a continuation of a cosmological force that imparts the relative momentum of the moving dimensional universe.

Enlightenment is to see the whole universe of environment, energy, and life, as one grand effort and behavior of a nonhuman-like cosmological force. The material form of the earth supports life that is a continuation of energy elements. Life draws sustenance for its relative motion and function from the whole. The human conscious willing self and the subconscious soul of each and all is a continuation of a cosmic procession of relative motion.

Trust

One of the mottos of the United States found on its currency is, "In God We Trust." In a god it is best not to trust, for it is evident that little care and protection exists for life except what humans can muster.

Better to trust in the ability and potential of a real conscious cerebral cortex and a subconscious triune soul. The human conscious self is a continuation of a subconscious soul that is a continuation of the earth. The triune soul is a forcible internal push to obtain food, have sex and reproduce, and to aggressively compete.

One fine day in the future of seeking truth, the whole truth, and nothing but the truth, in the United States a much more truthful motto might be adopted to state, "In the Metaphor of God We Trust."

Inflammation

Inflammation is an innate protective response by the immune system of the body to reduce or eliminate infection, irritants, or impact, and to stimulate cell and tissue repair. Acute inflammation is the first response to harm, while chronic inflammation occurs over time. Chronic inflammation can result in impaired health, injury and illness. Chronic or prolonged inflammation also leads to a condition of simultaneous cell destruction and healing. Too little response by the immune system and inflammation results in cell and tissue damage while over response causes harm known as auto-immune disorders.

Physical inflammation presents symptoms of pain, redness, heat, and swelling. Certain strains of viruses and bacteria cause systemic and topical inflammation. Sunburn is an inflammation. Mental and physical stress and poor diet cause cellular inflammation. Inflammation is a symptom of a lack of wellness and incipient illness. Serious and prolonged inflammation may result in impairment of cell and organ function and even death.

Similar to physical inflammation, there can be diagnosed a condition of psychological inflammation, and its symptoms are an inability to focus attention and to concentrate. This impairment usually results in the disorder and disability of an excess of picture images of past and future in the cerebral cortex of the brain.

Due to a lack of disciplined meditation, beginning in childhood, the human cerebral cortex of the brain develops a condition of psychological inflammation. Sensations of seeing, hearing, smelling, tasting, and touching are the fuel that often ignite into an excess of picture images and so inflame the brain. The picture images are predominantly of food, sex and reproduction, and aggression. The cerebral cortex of the brain becomes inflamed with picture images, and the body becomes inflamed with feverish willing for food, sex, and aggression.

Both conscious and subconscious attention must be trained in meditation. Meditation is the only effective way of reducing internal psychological inflammation of excess picture images and forcible and habitual willing behaviors.

Symptoms

Life is a symptomatic disease. Its symptoms consist of hunger for food, sex and reproduction, and aggression that spread the disease. Through the course of life the disease symptoms often subside but soon return.

In an attempt to ameliorate the disease of living, rabbis, priests, ministers, and imams display a higher level of behaviors toward lay humans and the situations of life. Religious authorities imitate and act for a first father god. The imagined first father cared to make life, and especially humans. Human advocates for the first father then imitate the god by exhibiting the behaviors of caring, patience, forbearance, love, kindness, service, and charity for human life. Monotheistic functionaries and adherents claim to act for a first father god but in reality act only on behalf of the elevating cerebral cortex of the human brain.

Medication

The great majority of humans medicate rather than meditate. A medication is defined as:

"A drug, remedy, or something that prevents or alleviates symptoms of discomfort or pain of physical disease, injury, or psychological disorder."

Some of the favored ways individuals medicate themselves to feel better is to indulge in alcohol, legal and illegal drugs, and to overindulge in consuming food, sex and reproduction, and aggression. A monotheistic first father god is also a widely used subjective and imaginary medicating idea, a nostrum that many use to protect themselves and to alleviate the varying pains of worry, loneliness, disease, injury, and dangers of living.

Meditation

The average person ignorantly thinks they are fully conscious and aware. This is definitely not the case in reality. Each person if only vaguely, indistinctly, or distinctly, see as real and yet realize the mirage of sensations, picture images of the brain, and willing for or against someone or something.

Only an exceptional person observes and disciplines the changing sensations of the senses, the picture images of the brain, and conscious and subconscious willing for or against. Individuals who consistently meditate seek to reduce the often cloud-like haze of associations, memories, and imaginations, and thereby to attain an increase clarity of perception. With consistent practice of meditation, the ability to focus and concentrate attention on a sensate object increases. There is a corresponding lessening of picture images that measure space and time. The ability to disengage attention from the cerebral cortex brain picture images of objects increases. The forcible triune soul of hunger for food, sex and reproduction, and aggression lessens.

During meditation, a stage is reached when conscious attention rests from sensations, and rests from picture images. Then can be better distinguished the animating triune soul of a forcible hunger for food, sex and reproduction, and aggression. The less conscious soul can then be observed and moderated to a conscious calm and subconscious poise.

Meditation reduces attention to sensations of seeing, hearing, smelling, tasting, and touching. Meditation reduces the proliferation of picture images of now, past, and future, and reduces excessive willing for food, sex and its byproduct of reproduction, and aggression.

What occurs in conscious self brain awareness are sensations, picture images, and forcible willing of hunger for food, sex and reproduction, and aggression. The brain organizes sensations of objects and places them in a space-time sequence of images. Meditatively observed to be primary to secondary scenic images, is a forcible willing for food, sex and reproduction, and aggression.

The individual must train conscious attention and so develop the ability to focus, sort through, and reduce the miasma of picture images and willing by focusing attention on a particular repetitive sensation such as breathing. Meditating on the internal sensations of breathing reduces attention to internal picture images of now, past, and future.

The cerebral cortex of the brain transforms sensations of seeing, hearing, smelling, tasting, and touching, into picture images of space-time. Focusing meditative attention on the single internal sensation of breathing, reduces the flow of picture images. Attention rests from the continual perceptual picture making of conscious thinking and subject-object picture images in the brain.

The meditator does not get bored or fall asleep but instead sustains attention even into stages of subconscious light sleep.

In this way, levels or stages from conscious to less conscious and to subconscious is revealed to conscious attention.

Relationships reduce available time that can be better spent on training a focus of attention and meditative observation. Meditation reduces the distractions of imagining and associations, and calms the twin forces of attraction and aggression. If fortunate, the clarity of seeing and feelings of joy and success more than make up for required deprivation and necessary time spent alone.

Self and Soul Meditation

The proper goal of those who meditate, is to better distinguish and to comprehend the conscious self and subconscious soul. Through meditation practice, an individual can better observe and comprehend conscious sensations and brain processes of perception and conception, subconscious dreams, and autonomic body functions.

Excessive daily efforts to obtain food, to acquire sex and to reproduce and care for children, and efforts of aggression, reduce the effort to acquire self and soul knowledge. Preoccupation with physical objects, busy relationships, and the toil of work, are detrimental, destructive, and even lethal obstacles to conscious self, and less conscious and subconscious soul exploration. Yet with effort an individual can be successful in better comprehending the self and soul.

It must be observed and comprehended that sensations of seeing, hearing, smelling, tasting, and touching are continually changing, as are picture images of now, past, and future. The individual meditator directs attention to observe the image making function of the brain/mind that places objects in a space-time sequence, and that willing for and against objects is continually changing.

There is no long lasting pleasure or enduring satisfaction in the sensations of seeing, hearing, smelling, tasting, and touching.

There is no long lasting pleasure or enduring satisfaction in the picture images of now, past, or future. There is no long lasting pleasure or enduring satisfaction in willing for or against. There is no long lasting pleasure or enduring satisfaction in the triune soul as forcible hunger for food, sex and reproduction, and aggression.

Dark Secret

What is best (Greek aristos, arête to excel) in life is to comprehend the conscious self and subconscious soul. Through the diligent practice of meditative observation, exertion of the forcible subconscious soul is lessened. This has long been a dark secret and difficult to comprehend. Not to direct attention and not to observe body and brain, is to not be saved from the triune soul and the round of birth and death. Humans do not have to have their soul saved, humans must be saved from the soul, must un-save the soul. As a continuation of the energy of the earth and a cosmological force, the soul is saved by default.

For the mass majority of humans there is a failure to practice observation and to increase knowledge. Pulled to and fro by uncertainties and the sufferings of life, many fail to direct attention and to observe the distinction of the conscious self and subconscious soul. There is then a consequent failure to reduce the forcible triune soul of hunger for food, sex and reproduction, and aggression. Consequently, there is a return to the hellish earth of space and time existence. Then ensues the recurring struggle for nourishment, sex and reproduction, and aggression.

Saved Soul

An authentic soteriological meditation seeks not to save the soul but to save the individual from the soul by reducing and moderating the triune forcible hunger for food, sex and reproduction, and aggression. True meditation serves to save the individual from a destruction-resistant soul that continues to persist and recur.

Modern science reveals the essence of the environment and life to be circular and radiant energy. The animating soul is a continuation of a cosmological force and earth element energy, and therefore has a trait of long lastingness in which coheres a subconscious forcible pattern of hunger for food, sex and reproduction, and aggression, along with remnant picture images that cohere to a habitual pattern of willing.

Humans are always going, going for food, for sex and reproduction, and for thoughts, words, and behaviors of aggression. This conscious intended activity lays down subconscious habit patterns. As a continuation of the energy of the earth, and a cosmological force, the habit pattern is resistant to destruction.

Humans share an origin as a continuation of the earth environment and an unmeasurable cosmological force. Life is a continuation of both element energy of the earth and a cosmological force that moves the universe. The individual soul is a continuation of the environment as a forcible hunger for food, sex and reproduction, and aggression that forces life to live and survive. As a continuation of energy and force the animating soul is resistant to destruction.

Human behavior is related to the behavior of the environment. Only in imaginary story is human behavior related to the behavior of a first father god. The human soul recurs as a continuation of the cycles of the earth environment of day and night, weather, and seasons. As nature or the environment is repetitive, so is the triune soul that is a continuation of it. The universe consists of repetitive solar, planetary, lunar, and galactic orbits that endure for countless millennia. The entire cosmos repeats through countless cycles of appearing and disappearing numberless galaxies.

There is a repetitive procession of endless days and nights and repeating seasons of the earth. Repetitive human habits and the repetitive ritual behaviors of religion subconsciously imitate the repetitive and relative comfort of the environment.

Life is often a disorderly willful struggle to develop, obtain, and to maintain order or to inflict disorder. Not consciously observing this to be so through meditation, acquired subconscious habits want to hold on to and repeat and so having died to return to the fray of life. The subconscious forceful habits of an individual returns through the shortcut of a developing fertilized egg and fetus. Human souls may recur to animate another body and to assemble with other souls on the earth to again search for answers to the internal and external endless problems of living.

The evidence of many cases of near death experiences exist in the files of researchers on the topic, in journal articles, and in published books. Childhood claims of reincarnation have been extensively investigated by Ian Stevenson (1918-2007) and other researchers. But no evidence or studies exist for a claimed resurrection of a deceased person by a first father god. Yet many monotheists insist they have a first father god who they think will save the body from oblivion by one day in the future resurrecting it. The physical body of the deceased will not be resurrected or remade by a monotheistic first father god who cares for humans. Since a monotheistic first father god is an artistic imaginary way of identifying the beginning of existence, and a way of obtaining care and protection, there will never be a resurrection of the human body.

In reality, it is the animating triune soul that will resurrect from the physical body of the earth to another dimension of existence. As some case studies and anecdotal evidence suggests, the animating soul may return to live as another physical body; a reincarnation. All bodies from subatomic quantum particles, atoms, and electrons to planets, stars, and galaxies move in a circular direction. As a continuation of a cosmological force and energy, an animating triune force of a soul must follow a similar trajectory.

Beginning and ending beget each other. The seen and unseen universe is an organization of circles from the smallest quantum particles to the largest galaxies. Mimicking the behavior of the cosmos, life and death are a circular continuation of omnipotent and omnipresent cosmological cycles.

Soul

It must be a seemingly boundless and destruction resistant animating triune soul that gives the sense of a free will in humans. Yet the soul contrasts with and is bounded by time limits and constraints of the biological body.

The function of the soul is to animate, to increase, grow, and to push and extend the limits of biological function. As a continuation of earth elements of energy, and a cosmological force, a triune soul animates and moves life to its relative limits. Life is limited but what animates it is unlimited as a continuation of non-limited energy and a nonfinite cosmological force that ever exists on its own.

Of what else can life be a continuation? The animating triune soul is a long-lasting continuation of the energy elements of earth. Without a doubt, life is a continuation of relative energy of earth elements and cosmological force. The truth of the origin of life is certainly not contained in a fantastic artistically imagined tribal myth of a first father god. There is a single force that organizes all aggregates, and it is not childishly human-like in any way. A single cosmological force organizes stars and planets and on earth equally organizes clouds and living forms.

Soul and Meditation

As the universe goes on and on seemingly forever, so too do continuations of it such as energy and the human triune soul. Picture images of the brain may also be preserved in a coherent way as a continuum of an energy surround, a magnetic field, and a cosmological force.

Picture images or perceptions, are formed in the subconscious and rapidly or slowly enter conscious awareness. Subconscious brain functions convert sensations into conscious picture images so as to better obtain what it needs or wants. An accumulation of picture images are stored as memory.

This forms a habit soul that less consciously and subconsciously exists to survive through repetition. Since the animating soul is a continuation of the energy elements of the earth, and a cosmological force, it has the characteristics of being resistant to destruction and long-lasting.

The lazy do not discipline the triune forcible soul as it forces the cerebral cortex of the brain to make many picture images of food, sex, and aggression. In ignorant response to life situations and out of desperation, the cerebral cortex may then imagine and evoke a first father god to assist in the struggle inside the brain and body and outside with the environment.

For the average person the image making ability of the brain is undisciplined and uncontrolled. An incessant stream of conscious picture images as memory of past and future images and the less conscious primary triune soul of a forcible hunger for food, sex and reproduction, and aggression, distract and dominate now attention. A disciplined focus of attention during meditation reduces conscious picture images. Focus of attention may then be directed to reducing the forceful and less conscious triune soul.

Meditation is the practice of observing and acquiring knowledge of less conscious and subconscious brain and body functions. Consistent meditation practice of fixing attention reduces conscious picture images, and reduces the subconscious and dominant triune soul of hunger for food, sex and reproduction, and aggression. Meditative observation calms the picture images of the cerebral cortex of the brain and the repetitive habits of brain and body, and thereby calms repetition of life and death.

The word "think" or thinking, is a vague term that obscures the process of making picture images in the conscious cerebral cortex of the brain by placing objects in a space and a time sequence. This is the mind or "my in" of the conscious cerebral cortex of the brain, supported and directed by the less conscious and subconscious cerebellum, midbrain, organs, and cells of the body.

Prior to the evolution of the cerebral cortex and its ability to make picture images, the midbrain, plexuses, organs, and cells of the body received sensations of molecular and element energy from the environment and other living forms. The less evolved way of knowing by early hominin species and Homo sapiens was dominated by emotions and mood, and rudimentary intuitive impressions.

Thinking, or the continual making of conscious picture images is reduced during meditation. The result is an improved ability to focus attention, less distraction, and a clarity of perception. The meditating individual is not overly inundated with sensations of pleasures and pains, with picture images, and willing for or against. Observant and clear comprehension develops through consistent practice of meditation.

Wise

A wise person reduces participation in the distractions of a madhouse society. Utilizing meditation and a focus of attention, the wise reduce sensations of seeing and hearing from which excessive picture images of past memory or future are produced by the cerebral cortex of the brain.

The wise comprehend that society can be harmful to individual sensitivity and growth. The wise comprehend that Middle East and Western societies worship an artistically imagined first father god. The wise comprehend the soul, the animating and forcible hunger for food, sex and reproduction, and aggression. The wise glimpse the triune soul to be a continuation of and supported by the energy elements of the earth. The wise accept that all relative forms and motion are a continuation of a cosmological force that ever exists on its own.

Only by reducing the over-active daily life of society, can an individual calm attention to sensations, picture images of the cerebral cortex of the brain, and impulsive and over-active behaviors.

With eyes closed and quiet, an individual can meditatively observe the picture images that form in the cerebral cortex of the brain from sensations of the outside environment. Calming the image making process, an individual can then direct attention to better observe inside and outside, and the functions of the conscious and subconscious brain and body.

Sensations continually change moment to moment, picture images change, and conscious and subconscious behaviors of body change. Conscious change is the self, and subconscious change is the soul. In physical terms, there exists the conscious cerebral cortex of the brain and central nervous system, and the subconscious cerebellum, midbrain, autonomic nervous system, plexuses, organs, and cells of the body.

Fasting

Many people are mesmerized, yet are unaware of being in such a state. Most humans are mesmerized as they do not practice meditation. In the twentieth century, some theistic religions have spoken out against the practice of meditation, variously referring to it as "dangerous" and the "work of the Devil."

Many people do not meditate, that is, they do not reduce attention to sensations of external objects, and to a continual internal flow of picture images. When the brain makes an excess of picture images it becomes dysfunctional. When picture images are slowed during meditation, there is a tendency to sleep, and so most beginning mediators fall asleep. Humans may awake rested and refreshed but remain cognitively asleep lulled into a waking sleep by a continual stream of internal brain picture images of the external environment.

In the Gnostic Gospel of Thomas, logion 27, Jesus is portrayed as saying, "If you do not fast from the world, you will not find the kingdom."

To fast from the world is to not get excessively caught up in the distractions of life for food, sex, aggression, family, and possessions of all kinds. Not only must there be a fasting from material objects, there must also be a fasting of the cerebral cortex of the brain from picture images of objects derived from sensations of the senses.

The average cerebral cortex of the human brain is out of control with a continual stream, and at times, a flood of picture images. When picture images are reduced and calmed, an individual can better observe conscious brain processes. It may then be possible to observe that a first father god is an artistic conception of the cerebral cortex of the brain, and that the soul is a problem of living as a triune forcible hunger for food, sex and reproduction, and aggression. There can also be intuitively sensed that the triune soul is a continuation of the energy elements of the earth and further intuited to be a continuation of a cosmological force that permeates multiple dimensions of reality. At least one of these dimensions might well be a place for the energy and force of the triune soul to reside in a coherent way. Energy and animating force is a reality during life, and after life may continue to exist in a real coherent and stable state.

The universe is a phenomena of both order and disorder. When observing the rampant disorder of life, and lacking a physical refuge, some fearful humans seek a psychological refuge by imagining a first father beginning of the human line. Humans sense they are a continuation of the origin of order yet to explain it, wrongly conceptualize it to be a first father god.

Though the body becomes disordered through illness, injury, and ageing, humans have a trust that somehow despite the disorder of living, they will experience a meaningful and coherent order or restoration after physical death.

It is possible that the reported sensing of an afterlife dimension may be derived from dream images of the departed. Or, there may well be a sensing of a real dimension that exists as a continuation of the earthly dimension, a reality sensed through seeing, hearing, or feeling a coherent presence of the deceased person.

Some may sense that despite the disorder of the body and physical death, there is an unseen order existing in another dimension of reality, to which the energy and force of the body transits to exist. So many persons have anecdotally reported this spontaneous phenomenon of sensing the deceased that it cannot be simply attributed to grieving and hallucination.

Living humans may be able to communicate with the energy remnant of a deceased person. It might be possible to communicate with the conscious self and the subconscious soul of a deceased individual. Humans cannot communicate with what does not exist or with what exists only in subjective imagination such as a first father god that is a subjective artistic creation of the cerebral cortex of the human brain.

Save

The animating triune soul as a forcible hunger for food, sex and reproduction, and aggression, directs each individual life to survive. Life is a continuation of the supportive earth from which it originates, and the environment is a continuation of cosmological force and motion.

There is a direct continuation from the cosmological motion of the universe to the environment and the earth, and to the subconscious and conscious movement of life. The individual should be uplifted through life and the expectation of death by contemplating that existence is a direct continuation of the immortal mover of the universe, a cosmological force that ever exists on its own.

A first father god is only a clumsy metaphorical mechanism for making this great truth known. Artificially inserting a first father into a genealogical sequence of biological fathers is an artistic artifice, a false and expedient stratagem accepted by so many to be true. A universal first father god is only a utilitarian subjective artistic and imaginary first father beginning that furnishes protection during life and after death.

Picture images occur in the cerebral cortex of the brain. The cerebral cortex is secondary in size to and is supported by the primary cerebellum and midbrain of willing behaviors. The conscious picture images of positioned objects in a space-time sequence are a continuation of the subconscious animating triune soul.

Since brain picture images of the cerebral cortex are a continuation of the primary triune soul, some memory must also be saved after death of the physical body. Based on the physics theory of conservation of energy, at least some conscious picture images must be conserved and saved to exist as an extension of the subconscious forcible triune soul. The personal quest for objects in space and time images continues on as momentum of the long-lasting animating triune soul. Animation of the physical body ceases but as a continuation of animating earthly energy and as a continuation of cosmological force, the triune forcible soul continues as a coherent conscious and subconscious habit.

Any dimensions of energy and force must endure longer than those consisting of compound material forms. Generations of humans observe and comment on material forms of the environment to last thousands of years. Most living forms endure for a brief time. Life forms are observed to be pitiful as they are vulnerable to injury, illness, and ageing. Yet as pitiful as human life is, it is embedded in and is a continuation of the earth that consists of elements of energy. Humans are also embedded in and are a continuation of the greater motion of the universe and a cosmological force that ever exists on its own.

Feat

It is quite an easy feat to imagine and accept the tradition of a first father god who can assist an individual. It is an astounding difficult feat to observe individual brain and body functions and to successfully sort through the difficult maze of the conscious self and the subconscious soul.

The savior of an individual is not an imagined first father god, or his supposed only begotten son, or the supportive members of the monotheistic religion. The real savior is an animating triune soul. The long-lasting soul is good for survival but is bad and havoc creating through an individual life. The animating soul is not mortal and that is the problem with it. The problem of the soul is not to save it but to un-save it. The soul is destruction resistant as it is a continuation of the energy elements of the earth, and a cosmological force that ever exists on its own.

Buddha (circa 623-543 BCE) was not a prophet who spoke for a first father god that is subjectively imagined in the cerebral cortex of the brain. Buddha did not artistically imagine the beginning of the environment and life to be a first father god. He was an astute empirical observer of brain and body functions, following in the much older tradition of yoga.

Monotheists seek the beginning of existence by imagining it to be a first father god. While Hindus do have a plethora of artistically imagined gods and goddesses, they also searched for the origin of existence dwelling inside the body, supported by a real earth, and a cosmic expanse of space and a cause and effect sequence of time or karma.

What brings forth life was recognized but was not clearly articulated by an observant Buddha. He alluded to it indwelling the body by using the metaphor of a housebuilder. The *Dhammapada* is a collection of brief sayings accepted by tradition to be the actual words of the Buddha spoken by him at the time of his awakening:

"Verse 153: Through many lives I wandered, seeking but not finding the builder of this house; ill it is to be born again and again.
Verse 154: House-builder, you are seen, no house shall you build again! Rafters and ridge-pole are dismantled. My mind has reached the unconstructed; all constructing now stilled."

The maker and builder of life is not an imaginary first father god but a real supportive earth outside, and a real animating triune soul of life inside as a hunger for food, sex, and aggression.

Life is replete with many irritations that stimulate the mild or strenuous effort to recover or to maintain moderate balance. Waiting, boredom, disrespect, car trouble, poverty, crime, vandalism, ill health, conflict and arguments with family members, neighbors, and coworkers, and gossip and lies are just a few of life irritations.

With a consistent practice of meditation there may be an experience of what Buddha called nirvana. Nearing nirvana may be indicated during meditation and in general by an eventual lessening of irritations and a less wanting sensations of particular objects. There will also be observed to be a lessening and a not wanting picture images of objects, and there will be a lessening and not wanting to will for the objects that over time, to have or to hold, is usually futile. This observation suggests that an individual is at least on the path to and perhaps near to nirvana.

What makes something real are sensations of an object, picture images of an object, and willing for or against an object. To deemphasize the relative reality of an object, there must be a meditative lessening of wanting sensations, of wanting and constructing picture images, and lessening of willing for and wanting of an object.

Struggle

Struggle through existence is often made easier through lying. Humans have to frequently lie to themselves and others to get through life. Children lie to parents and adults, and parents lie to each other and to relatives, friends, coworkers, and to government authorities. Most lie so as to avoid or to reduce struggle with others.

Physical struggle begins with a sperm and egg in the dimension of the mother's womb and body, to develop and struggle and transit into birth.

Growing and maturing an individual struggles with family members and friends. Humans often struggle to get through the next conversation, the next meal, the next relationship. Humans seek to avoid or to at least have less struggle with health, money, and relationships.

Humans struggle with now, past, and future experiences. In the ever moving stream of time, many tired and confused in the struggle of living are swept into poverty, ill health, or psychological disorders. Adults struggle through life and a great many imagine a human-like first father god who will reduce or save them from struggle. To rely on an imaginary first father god is better than to overly rely on human help to save.

Some grasp onto the promoted idea of the beginning of existence to be a first father god. To reduce the struggle of daily life, many accept the theological prevarication of a first father god. Monotheists lie on a daily basis to themselves and to others about the beginning of existence. For many only the idea of a first father god makes life tolerable. For protection in life and death, many assemble in a group to position themselves under the protection of a shared and imagined first father god.

Many struggle to get through another day and night, and to get to a place where they will no longer struggle. Whoever wants to no longer struggle upon the earth or elsewhere, must turn to observe and learn more about life. The conscious and subconscious memory cluster of struggles during a lifetime, whether brief or chronic, most likely continue to exist as a continuation of a universe that perpetually exists in a multiverse of space-time dimensions of reality.

Dimensions of reality have not been made by a first father god. All dimensions of existence are a continuation of cosmological force. Each individual struggles not only in the context of an earthly dimension of the home, neighborhood, town, state, and country.

The individual struggle on earth occurs in a not usually cognized greater dimension of existence. Daily life upon the earth occurs in the greater reality of the solar system that occurs in the greater reality of the Milky Way galaxy that occurs as a continuation of millions of other galaxies. To struggle in one dimension of the earth is to struggle in the context of greater dimension of a multiverse.

Long-Lasting

The phenomenon of the universe, according to cosmologists, continues to be long lasting, perhaps as old as fourteen billion years and counting. Brief life is connected to the observed long-existing universe but it is usually not seen how this is so.

The fact of a long-lasting universe tends to lend credence and to confirm the continuing existence of the animating essence of individual life, the triune soul as a forcible hunger for food, sex and reproduction, and aggression. The force that invisibly moves the visible universe also moves invisibly within visible living forms.

The shedding of the accretion of the physical body from its essence of energy and animating force occurs at death. Only a very few humans perceive and comprehend that the animating essence of life, the triune soul, is not disconnected from elements of energy and a cosmological force of which it is a continuation. The triune soul is a long-lasting continuation of a long-existing universe.

The human cerebral cortex of the brain imagines and manufactures a first father god. It is much easier to imagine a first father god rather than to make the effort to comprehend the existence of an animating soul. Many have sought and most have failed to comprehend the soul. The highway of effort is littered with those who never arrived at their aspired destination of finding the soul. Instead, most take a detour in the direction of a disappointing dead end of a first father god.

Those who have failed to comprehend the animating soul of life are especially evident by individuals and cultures who direct attention away from inside the brain and body to an imagined outside first father god. The failure of individuals and cultures to comprehend the human soul, is compensated for by imagining a first father god. Monotheistic religions and cultures are symptoms of a cognitive failure to comprehend the triune soul of life.

The soul has for so long been doubted, overlooked, and misconceived, and clouded over with monotheistic superstition. The soul is not to be observed as an object in a particular location but can be observed as a dynamic of living. The triune soul as a forcible hunger for food, sex and reproduction, and aggression, is the innate mechanism of survival in an earthly dimension. Essential for life to survive in an earthly dimension, the triune soul may also insure continued survival to another dimension.

Souls are a continuation of the earth and the energy elements that compose it. Both life and the environment are a continuation of the motion of the universe, a cosmological force that ever exists on its own. The animating soul of life is a continuation of an unknown and inferred cosmological force, and yet is not comprehended to be so. Instead, the origin of life is projected outward and adorned with human attributes to be ideationally apparent as a first father god.

Personality Trait

While young and as adults, each attempts to better comprehend how life is to be lived by reasoned conscious choices. Each seeks to comprehend the conditions and circumstances of individual life, yet few seek to comprehend its essence. The essence of each individual life is a hunger for certain preferred foods, preferences for sex and reproduction, and aggressions. Dependent on the triune soul of hunger, sex, and aggression, each person tends to have a dominant personality trait. The average person is a combination of each trait.

A great many prefer food and also acquire oral habits of overeating, smoking, drinking, and digestive tract problems. Many more prefer to emphasize sex and spend much time pursuing sexual experience, relationships, and reproductive family life. Others prefer aggression and tend toward the military, legal system and police work, martial arts, and physical fitness. These triune animating traits are the main dynamic of behavior and of a bleak human history.

Animating Soul

The unreasoning and irrational soul directs the reasoning and rational self. In physical terms, the subconscious cerebellum, midbrain, and autonomic nervous system of the body directs the conscious cerebral cortex and central nervous system.

Overly forcing the less conscious body, the subconscious triune soul responds by forcibly causing psychosomatic symptoms of stress and disease. Yet the rational conscious self offers guidance and direction to the less rational and subconscious soul.

As a continuation of the earth, the triune soul is the animating essence of living forms. The animating essence of life from the smallest to the largest is the activating need for nourishment, sex and/or reproduction, and aggression. The soul is a continuation of the forcible energy elements of the supportive earth, moon, and sun environments. In turn, all relative movement and motion of the universe is a continuation of a cosmological force, field, or ground that ever exists on its own.

Act of Force

The animating force to act of living creatures is nestled in and supported by, and is a continuation of the energy elements of the environment. The energy elements and motion of the forms of the environment are a continuation of a cosmological force. Forced to act and react by the outside environment and forced on the inside by the triune soul, humans chronically suffer.

Humans suffer from a real environment, other living forms, and equally suffer from a real animating triune soul of hunger for food, sex and reproduction, and aggression.

Each individual is forced to act and react by both outside conditions and by functions inside the body. Pain and agitation enter from the external environment through sensations of the senses. External sensate pleasures do not last and are reduced or cease through change; therefore are soon dissatisfying.

Few individuals are successful in avoiding or fending off agitation and pain inflicted by the external environment and the pain of loss of objects that bring pleasure. Even fewer manage to fend off internal sensations of pain and agitation caused by the forcible triune soul of hunger, sex, and aggression. Less intelligent humans of the past as well as those living in modern times, imagine an intelligent first father who made intelligent life and the environment. Humans suffer in life not from a real god but suffer needlessly from the false hope of an imaginary first father god.

Vision

If for a brief time humans could have visual acuity that can see energy, the solid appearing earth will be seen as glowing elements of atoms, electrons, protons, neutrons, and subatomic quantum particles. All waters will be seen as drops, pools large and small, as streams of shifting and flowing atoms and electrons of H2O. Air will seem as shimmering atoms and electrons of oxygen, nitrogen, carbon dioxide, and other gases. The light and temperature of the sun will be seen to be composed of animated photons of light and infrared and ultraviolet wavelengths.

Stars, planets, and moons will be seen as shimmering seas of atoms and electrons. The human body will be seen to be composed of energy, atoms and electrons of various elements glowing and pulsating with the force of life. Only then will the body and brain be clearly seen to be a continuation of the earth and solar environments.

Living bodies are supported by and are an energy continuation of the environment and are an active outgrowth of it. Readily apparent to eyes capable of seeing energy particles, will be that life has an origin and birth from the planet, and that the ingredients of life are a continuation of the earth. Perhaps only with enhanced visual ability, will it be better comprehended that a first father god is an artistic imagination that clouds clear comprehension of energy and forces of the universe.

Humans need to know where the environment and life comes from, need more intelligence, and need help living, dying, and after death. This is why a first father god is imagined and projected to exist. Imagining the events of the environment and human experience to be the result of the thoughts of a first father god is but a utilitarian delusion at best.

Limited Intelligence

Human intelligence is limited by various conditions. Gene expression and genetics have a role in limiting individual intelligence. Research has shown this to be true of chimpanzees as well as humans.

Neuroscience research finds in general that the human brain does not fully mature in cognitive ability and intelligence until twenty-five years of age. Beginning near forty-five years the ability of the ageing brain to remember and reason begins to decline. Mature learning and reasoning is generally limited to a mere twenty years.

Conscious function of the cerebral cortex of the brain is also limited by the subconscious cerebellum, midbrain, autonomic nervous system, and body. Since the origin of the conscious self is the subconscious soul, there is a continual intrusion of the less conscious triune soul into functions of the conscious self. There is limited attention and observation of cognitive functions of both the conscious self and the subconscious soul.

This limitation occurs by not practicing meditation, the result of which is a lack of individual ability to focus attention and to better comprehend. Without a practice of meditation, individual attention is easily distracted. Not able to focus attention, a person has little ability for perception and instead relies on conceptions and emotional preferences for or against varying situations and ideas.

Cognitive limitations make up the average handicap of unequal human comprehension. Cognitive limitation is the best condition and overall climate for the seed thoughts of monotheism to be planted and sprout into the blind growing but unknowing plant of faith, belief, and tradition. For many, monotheism is a persistent and pleasant delusion. A nonvisible first father god is an easy way to impose a simple orientation to an unknown beginning, to proffer protection and care, and to establish authority and social order.

Average

To locate and to get closer to the origin of all things, the average individual must accept the poor and worn idea that the beginning of the environment and life is a first father god. The average person may also join with others in a monotheistic religious service with its various rituals. The average busy person may even study and learn some of the religion's teachings but mostly at a superficial level of comprehension.

A human-like god is an imagined pointer in the direction of what is good, a first father and another dimension. Some average individuals seek to escape biological life and the earth dimension When the Romans executed Jesus and the two thieves, they went to Paradise the same day. (Luke 23:43) In his teachings, Jesus spoke of escape from the earthly dimension to another dimension. However, Jews, most Christians, and Muslims do not escape from the earth when they die. The body has to rest or sleep until resurrection by the god. There is no escape of a soul to another dimension.

The direction of good is imagined by many to be a first father god, a mere word symbol to indicate the way to a human-like imaginary good that can intend care and protection. For many there is no other greater good that can be imagined than a first father god. In the Genesis story there is a focus on the origin of all things and much attention to a special human beginning. The focus on the specialness of humans who are directed to subdue all things (Genesis 1:28) is mere egocentric attention by humans to humans. A first father god is an imagined ego with which to surround the average human ego.

There is some meager utilitarian good in paying attention to the daydream of an imagined first father god. The god identifies the beginning of existence, and provides supportive care and protection. In contrast, what is observably real is a much better good, such as attention to the cosmological motion of the universe, and attention to how the earth is the origin of and is supportive of life. Only in subjective imagination is a first father god supportive of human life.

A non-average good is to comprehend what the animating soul of life really is, a forcible hunger for food, sex and reproduction, and aggression, the hellish cause of biological existence. To reduce and to be relatively free of these subconscious compulsions, is to approach a higher good.

It is a great non-average good to reach the comprehension that the animating soul of life is a continuation of the earth, and that the environment is a continuation of a cosmological force. It is an exalted good to reach the comprehension that there exists another dimension of existence and as anecdotal and case study evidence of childhood reincarnation suggests, a return to the earthly dimension.

Gauntlet

The word gauntlet is defined as:

"A punishment in which a sufficient number of people armed with sticks or weapons form two long lines facing each other. The individual being punished is forced to run from one end of the lines to reach the other end while being forcibly hit, and often spit upon and called names."

Each individual is clubbed throughout the gauntlet of life on both sides by accidents, disease, poverty, and mistreatment and harm by fellow humans. The gauntlet of life also consists of enduring the clubbing of wanting to have, and on the other side wanting not to have, with only brief respites taken. This is the inevitable tortuous run and conflict through the gauntlet of life. Each having been conceived and then born, must endure the run of life as best they can. Any attempt to escape the gauntlet of life is futile.

A greater force for an average individual is a real human hero. Greater than a hero is the collective force of a real human group. Greater than any individual or group is the artistically imagined first father god of monotheism that serves to explain the origin of existence. The first father god can then be appealed to for care and protection through the real gauntlet of both life and death.

Soul and Resurrection

An imagined first father god originates in the conscious cerebral cortex of the brain, and also represents it. In monotheistic religions an imagined first father god takes precedence. The fault in monotheistic religions is that they plaster over the universe with the imagined first father god. In so doing they overlook a real animating triune soul.

Humans differ from the biblical first father god who knows how to form the environment and life. Humans first obtained only rudimentary knowledge placed in humans by the first father, and later obtained some extra unauthorized knowledge for themselves in the Garden of Eden. Breathing into humans, the god began the respiration of life. However, most importantly, the god made the first humans to be soulless.

In the Genesis story, the human body is made only from soil, and there is no immortal part existent within humans that was derived from the god. Therefore, the god must reassemble humans during a resurrection, a raising of many a dead body.

Correcting the omission of not creating humans with a soul, is the main message of the gospel or "good news" that the northern Israelite Jesus taught to the southern tribe of Judah. The notion that the physical body will be resurrected is primitive Jewish thinking. In contrast, the good news of the Christian message is that there is an afterlife place of "many mansions" (John 14:2) to be with others in paradise. For Jesus there was no waiting for a resurrection, only an ascension into an afterlife. "And Jesus said unto him, Verily I say unto thee. Today shalt thou be with me in paradise." (Luke 23:43)

The earliest gospel of Mark as found in the Sinaiticus Codex was copied and written circa 330-360 CE. Chapter 16 of the gospel contains only eight verses. To later versions of the gospel of Mark, scribes and/or editors added an additional twelve spurious verses that include the physical resurrection of Jesus. The evidence is convincing that since there is no mention of a physical resurrection by the Christian writer of the earlier version of the gospel, there was a break from the tradition of Jewish resurrection.

The earlier Mark gospel does not include the resurrection of Jesus, and therefore contradicts the body resurrection teaching of the Jews. This convincingly points out the radical difference between the good news gospel of the northern Israelite Jesus and southern Jewish theology.

Monotheists take refuge in an imagined first father god, who making all things, must know all about the environment and life. However, the god of the Jews obviously did not know how to make a soul as he neglected to do so. In the thinking and believing of the Semitic Middle East, humans are dependent not on an animating soul but on a first father god to resurrect the physical body. The Semitic sects of Christianity and Islam also accept the view of body resurrection.

Some Christian denominations are influenced by Greek thinking that humans have a psyche or soul. Yet this soul will be reinstalled in the original physical body during its eventual resurrection. Modern Christians mistakenly of course, think of the soul as fully conscious and rational, like the imagined first father god.

Readily evident is that the physical body can be killed and will soon decay and rot. Not so evident is that what animates it is resistant to destruction. Those who accept reincarnation accept that the soul resurrects, yet only in a different body. Many peoples such as the Celts, Greeks, and Romans accepted this view, as do the Hindus and Buddhists of today. There exist many anecdotal and investigated case studies of reincarnation but to date none at all on even a single case of resurrection from a decaying or long dead body.

Perfection

The subconscious midbrain and body animated by a dynamic triune soul, has evolved the conscious and less than perfect cerebral cortex of the brain. Middle East monotheistic religions imagine a perfect beginning, and then explain how life became imperfect. However, life does not have a beginning from a perfect first father god. Imperfect humans have evolved from an imperfect environment.

Supported by and as a continuation of a less than perfect earth environment, humans have evolved, continue to survive as a species, and live a less than perfect life. As a continuation of earth energy, the less than perfect triune soul of hunger for food, sex and reproduction, and aggression, evolved the less than perfect cerebral cortex of the brain to better survive.

The subconscious soul of the midbrain and body evolved the conscious self of the cerebral cortex that must adjust to the animating soul inside of the body, and to the outside environment.

Overwhelmed and lacking real help and reliable advice, monotheistic adherents utilize their cerebral cortex of the brain to imagine the origin of existence to be a first father god who can be subjectively relied upon.

Society emphasizes the cerebral cortex and its ability to reason and measure reality. Society also emphasizes the ability of the cerebral cortex to imagine the artistic product of a forefather god. The view of a first father god is a delusion for over half of the earth's population. An individual either looks up to a real authority on the earth, or imagines an unreal authority of a first father god.

Not accurately perceived as a continuation of the environment, the human soul is viewed by Middle East derived monotheistic religions as nonexistent. The animating soul of life is not recognized to exist and human biological life must be saved by imagining a human-like god who will remake or resurrect the body. This view promotes individual helplessness and patriarchal dependency.

For early Jews, the dead journeyed to Sheol or the pit. There the shadows of the dead remained until the living forgot about them and they then vanished into nothingness. Later Jews thought of the unanimated body of the dead to be sleeping (2 Kings 14:16, Daniel 12:2, Job 14:12) until the god Yhwh reanimates, remakes, or resurrects it. Later Christians and Muslims also adopt this superstition and distorted way of thinking.

Contrast

The first father of the biblical Genesis story is a harsh god who cursed and banished the first humans. The god also destroyed most of life upon the earth with a flood. (Genesis 6, 7) The patriarch Abraham nearly killed his son Isaac when the god directed him to do so. (Genesis 22) According to Christian teachings, the same fatherly god allowed mere humans to kill his son Jesus as a sacrificial lamb. (1 Peter 1:19)

The Christian first father allowed his mutilated son to hang on a cross so that his shed blood would then avert the punishment to be meted out to humans after death by the punitive god. Who would want a first father like this?

Contrast and compare the Middle East sad scenario of horror stories with the gentle smile of personal fulfillment sculpted on the face of Siddhartha Gautama, better known to history as the Buddha, the awakened one. He achieved his exalted status by his own effort without the assistance of an imagined first father god.

In the countries of Myanmar and Thailand there are thousands of temples, pagodas, and sculptures of Buddha gilded with gold and inlaid with precious stones and diamonds. These were given to honor the accomplishment of awakening to reality. What a contrast with the mythic and metaphorical fantasies of monotheistic religions.

Father

Christian priests and ministers encourage use of and are often referred to by the term "father." These sacerdotalists represent the first father god. Catholic priests practice celibacy and have no biological family. They can then more easily function as a father figure of the church family members. The church fathers like to consider themselves just as important if not more so than the biological fathers of nuclear families.

The metaphorical mention of a first father god encourages acceptance of others as full family members. A shared first father is a basic handy way of including others. Yet the human condition is such that as the worn cliché states, "Familiarity breeds contempt." Both religious and biological families experience interpersonal conflict and sorrow.

The existence of a first father god imagined by the conscious cerebral cortex of the brain is secondary to the primary subconscious functions of the midbrain and autonomic nervous system of the body.

These primary biological functions are the life sustaining functions of an animating triune soul as a forcible hunger for food, sex and reproduction, and aggression.

The shortsighted cerebral cortex of the monotheistic Jews, Christians, and Muslims, does not bother to contemplate the animating functions of the body and instead settles on an ancestral first father as the maker of the environment and the animator of life. The human cerebral cortex is the animator of a simple cartoonish story of a first father god that animates life. However, life is not animated by a first father god but by a triune soul as a forcible hunger for food, sex and reproduction, and aggression, as a continuation of the environment. So shall it be for evermore.

Connection

The English word religion (Latin re, again, and ligare or ligio, to connect) literally means to reveal or establish a cognitive connection with where things come from. Monotheistic authorities actively insist on and promote the delusion that humans are connected to a first father god.

Atheists and scientists are correct in that there is no real human-like god but based at least on super string theory, there exists dimensions other than the earthly one. In the universe, each part is connected to another, and really to all parts as the physics theory of quantum entanglement or interconnectedness convincingly demonstrates with experiments. Each part of life is connected to the environment and vice versa.

Unfortunately, many humans like to imagine they are connected to a first father god. A first father god is what the human brain/mind subjectively imagines and is where attention can be directed to what is good. This is an artistic and imaginary way of getting beyond the real good and evils of earth.

Empirical science is an observational way of detecting what the environment and life is connected to. The cosmological explanation of what the environment and life is connected to, is the Big Bang explosion. Yet this scientific theory is not comforting to many.

The limiting ignorance of a first father origin is much more appealing, comforting, and easily comprehended than is comprehending the origin of the universe to be a great explosion. Therefore, monotheistic religion with its first father god continues to convince many.

Lowest To Highest

The view of monotheistic religions is that all things of the environment and life come from the higher intelligence of a single first father god. Yet, theistic religion has it backwards. What is higher did not make what is lower. What is lower has made what is higher.

The lowest is a nonhuman-like cosmological force. It is so low, it does not even appear as an object or phenomenon. Energy is a relative continuation of cosmological force and is so low that it has only been detected in modern times as elements, atoms, electrons, and ever finer subatomic quantum particles. These have an origin from a cosmological force, field, or ground that ever exists on its own.

Atoms and electrons of elements of energy cluster to form the lower supportive material forms of the environment of stars, planets, and moons. The lower level soil and water of earth supports the origin of life. Life is a continuation of a lower nonconscious environment of energy. The material environment has evolved life and the subconscious animating soul of hunger for food, sex and reproduction, and aggression.

The lower subconscious function of the body, autonomic nervous system, midbrain, and cerebellum of the brain has supportively evolved the higher cerebral cortex of the human brain.

The cerebral cortex reaches for the highest by going in the direction of the beginning and many humans imagine their origin to be a first father god. This way of thinking of course forms the Jewish, Christian, and Islamic monotheistic conundrum; how from the highest good has come the lower behaviors of humans.

The primitive folk mode of thinking that is monotheistic religion, does not examine what is lower or unseen. This task has fallen to science to find through observation and testing that from the lowly unseen has evolved what is larger and higher. From small atomic and subatomic particles have come the great size of the stars, planets, moons, and countless galaxies. From very small essential amino acids and bases, proteins, and minerals of carbon and selenium, and vitamins, have evolved living forms. From lowly microscope non-cellular viruses and cellular bacteria have evolved other multicellular living forms.

To say the environment and life has come from a higher intelligence of a human-like god is the worst of cognitive aberrations and is an outright delusion and a fraud on human comprehension.

Fashioning God

Humans generally rely on each other's higher intelligence located in the cerebral cortex of the brain. Monotheistic humans also rely on the imagined higher intelligence of a first father god, and this idea also occurs in the cerebral cortex of the brain.

A first father higher god originates in the highest and most conscious part of humans, the cerebral cortex of the brain. Humans have subjectively imagined and projected the god from their own brain to act as if it were an objective outside presence. A first father god is only and completely a subjective human way of knowing a beginning of the environment, life, and humans. The beginning is artistically imagined, and fashioned into a story of a Jewish, Christian, and Islamic fatherly god.

The Jews and Muslims fashion their god with words and story sans any visible images. The Christian religion also follows in this tradition yet has strayed from it in recent times. The Catholic church commissioned the sculptor and painter Michelangelo (1475-1564) to portray the first father god in a fresco ceiling painting in the Sistine Chapel. The god appears as a hoary old man signifying the first father or forefather of humankind. The god is shown almost touching fingers with Adam the first human. Jesus as the son of the god, is also portrayed in a fresco painting on the Chapel walls. The scene is of Jesus handing a key to the disciple Peter for the kingdom of heaven. (Matthew 16:19)

The Jews have their first father god who made the body of the first human from the earth to which all bodies will return. There is no soul that survives physical death, and only the first father god can remake the body. Since the god is an artistic imagining, the human body will never be resurrected. The commanding god of the Jews has to resurrect the biological bodies of his created progeny. In contrast, the fatherly Israelite god of Jesus has made a special afterlife to which his followers transition (John 14:2). Christianity is a crazy theological hodgepodge of both these views.

Fiction Bestseller

A god revealed to humans and recorded in writing is an artistic inspired expression of human imagination. A first father god is a poor portrayal of a beginning sequence, and is only an egocentric arrogance and a way to focus attention on the special status of humans.

The biblical Garden of Eden story portrays the first two humans as wanting to know more, to have more knowledge. This is the only miniscule truth in the otherwise fictional Genesis story. The basis of the fictional story is wanting to know more about the beginning of existence, and the Genesis story is the creative artistically imagined answer. The simple solution to the origin of existence is to imagine a forefather with amazing knowledge and strength.

The strength of a first father god also serves to strengthen the human resolve to live despite the numerous hardships of life.

The Jewish god's knowledge was obviously limited as he knew only how to make a life of the physical body and did not know how to fashion an animating soul. Therefore, the first father made his first two humans to have a soulless body. Based on the writings of Judaism, Christianity, and Islam, the god will have to remake the dead bodies of their descendants during a future resurrection.

In the Garden of Eden story, the special status of humans is spoiled by wanting to exceed the basic god endowed knowledge. The first humans endowed themselves with special god-like knowledge by eating a fruit. With this event the higher knowing god entered into conflict with willful lower knowing humans. The immediate higher knowledge that humans brought upon themselves by acquiring and eating the fruit was nudity, and how to create human life through sexual intercourse. The first two humans were then punished by the god with having to provide their own food for an ever recurring hunger that often leads to aggression among brotherly humans. (Genesis 4:8)

In the biblical Genesis tale, the cerebral cortex of the brain is externalized and portrayed in story to be an independent character of an intelligent first father god. The punishment inflicted on the first two humans by the portrayed god is the innate triune soul of life, a punishing forcible hunger for food, sex and reproduction, and aggression. The triune soul is viewed as punishment rather than what it truly is, an animating essence resistant to destruction.

The portrayed god is an elevating fiction of the cerebral cortex of the brain, and the animating triune soul is downgraded to fictional curses and punishment. The lower triune soul is offensive to the higher cerebral cortex of the brain. In physical terms, the unthinking lower cerebellum, midbrain, and body, offends the thinking higher cerebral cortex of the brain.

Humans make the beginning of existence known by lauding praises on a first father god. In monotheistic religions, truth wears a metaphorical disguise of a first father god. A first father god is a make-believe causal agent of simplistic human comprehension portrayed as a nonfiction story.

Any story portraying a first father god is an untrue fiction. The storied Bible and Quran are the number one fictional best sellers of all time. All gods are subjectively real but not objectively real. Santa Claus, the Easter bunny, tooth fairy, unicorns, and gods are subjectively and artistically real as imagined ideas but not objectively real.

Why do humans bother to read fiction? The answer is that fiction books are often entertaining, and they are also a way to escape the nonfiction of living which is all too often uninteresting, uncertain, boring, hazardous, and harmful.

Plato

Plato (circa 424–347 BCE) taught that works of art such as sculpture and paintings are secondary images derived from primary images occurring in conscious attention. Plato called the primary images the eidos or ideas. He thought the eidios are eternal or long lasting and exist in a realm of their own separate from the physical, and when not distracted the psyche can become conscious of them. This he thought, is the life and work of the philosopher.

Plato is in an error state when he regards the eidos or picture images of the cerebral cortex of the brain to be the psyche or soul. Picture images are secondary phenomena to a primary animating essence of life that is long lasting. Plato downgraded the appetites of hunger for food and aggression. Realistically, the animating soul is the forcible appetite for food, sex and reproduction, and aggression. The triune soul is a subconscious transformative habit of repetition and long lastingness.

Plato was intrigued by the ethereal mental images of the cerebral cortex of the brain. He was a mathematician and might have vaguely sensed how conscious mental images are measures of a space and time dimension. Plato thought the ability for images was the psyche or soul. However, the psyche or soul does not exist as an image or an object but rather as a dynamic animating essence as a forcible hunger for food, sex and reproduction, and aggression.

Picture images develop in the cerebral cortex of the brain from sensations of the senses while the cerebellum, midbrain and body intends experience animated by the triune soul. Most conscious experience of life is spent in obtaining and eating food, seeking or having sex, reproducing, and caring for its results, and expressing aggression in competition with others through use of words and behaviors.

Forcible sex and reproduction is the animating essence of life coequal with forcible hunger for food and aggression. Having no food, no sex and reproduction occurs, and with no effort and aggression, no life survives. Hunger for food, sex and reproduction, and aggression are the animating triune force of the soul.

Truth Upside Down.

Monotheists turn truth upside down. In Christian theological thinking, the human soul is regarded as the highest part and function of the human body. This is an intellectual bias that is a reversal of what is true.

The soul is the lowest as it is a continuation of the environment, and it forces life to live and to continue. The soul is the lowest subconscious function of the body, not the highest. The highest conscious function is the cerebral cortex of the brain that imagines a higher more intelligent first father to be a god to humans.

Games

Playing a game of cards is seeking to manipulate the order of cards through skill, luck, or chance, so as to get a sequence of a winning hand. Card games of chance and the consequent order of winning and disorder of losing, mirror the chance, order, and disorder of life.

A general estimation based solely on observation is that life works out to winning about sixty percent of the time, and losing forty percent of the time. Therefore a person has a slight edge to win and this tenuous edge is sufficient to encourage most people to continue to struggle making daily choices through life. The order that exists is from the standpoint of cause and effect, perfect. The environment is perfect and so is life.

Humans want to perfect what is seen by humans to be an imperfect existence, yet what is good is always accompanied by what is bad. Fun and pleasure last only so long and then sadness and pain inevitably occur. A forty percent average of disorder in life is disheartening yet is probably close to how the odds work out through an average lifetime. Humans lose at physical and mental health, lose a job or money, lose possessions, and lose supportive relationships through divorce, estrangement, and hostility.

An imaginary first father god serves to subjectively increase personal order and optimism in life but only manages to weakly reinforce and bolster individual effort and confidence enough to get through another objective day of living. Both a monotheistic god and a trusted and true friend make life easier. Assistance in life can be easily obtained by utilizing the cerebral cortex of the brain to imagine a first father god. A real trusted and true friend is much more difficult to find.

Order and Disorder

Humans use up much time in life attempting to make things orderly and to prevent disorder. This is a mostly full time occupation of living as order sooner or later changes to disorder. Generally speaking, life is a disorder.

While orderly, the dynamic of life proceeds inevitably to the disorder of illness, injury, ageing, and death. Life is both a benign order and a malignant disorder. Human reality is a delicate alternating balance of order and disorder and each individual orders life as best they can. The real worth of a human choice is not ascertained by a first father god but by how much order and good or disorder and bad it causes.

The order of life is either slowly or suddenly punctuated with disorder and a consequent effort to remove disorder and to restore order. In the experience of the average person, order usually prevails over disorder. Yet each is vulnerable to disruption of earthly life by many and varied physiological and psychological disorders.

That life is a duality of both order and disorder is an old observation. The prophet Zoroaster (circa 1200 BCE) declared that life is connected to the twin spirits of the good Ahura Mazda and the evil Ahriman. Zoroaster anthropomorphized both order and disorder into human-like causes. This thinking directly influenced the Semitic monotheistic religions of Judaism, Christianity, and Islam, to accept both a good human-like god and an evil Satan, Lucifer, Devil, or Iblis.

The fragile order of individual life is vulnerable to disorder from the environment and from other living forms. Humans in all cultures have sacrificed the lives of many individuals to influence the environment to be orderly, such as to bring rain, and to induce crops to grow. Evil or excessive force and consequent disorder is inflicted by the environment, living forms, and also by humans. To control disorder of the environment, disease, animals, and other humans in modern times, many continue to follow the primitive tradition of imagining a first father god. Others turn to a much more sane science.

If an individual is fortunate in life to escape serious illness and injury, all too soon arrives ageing and degeneration of the body and brain.

There has to be something that can repair the disorder of life. The monotheistic view is that only the maker of a perfect order can repair the disorder of life and after life. Many have faith that the biblical god who first created the sequence of perfect earthly order can easily restore earthly disorder to order. Yet, since monotheism is a mere artistic expression, the first father god never acts to improve the disorders of daily life on the earth.

A benign orderly life made by the first father god as told in the biblical Garden of Eden story, soon became malignant and disordered with the human acquisition of godly knowledge. Humans were first made with a basic knowledge endowed by the god but obtained godly knowledge from a tree, symbolic of nature or the environment. Since the time the first humans caused disorder, each individual descendent continues to cause their own order and disorder of life.

A biblical perfect first father god wrought only an orderly good. He provided food, created humans with sexual organs and yet the god wisely made them inactive, and no aggression existed in the Garden of Eden. Then came imperfection and what is bad or evil, a disorder wrought by humans when they obtained knowledge of sex and reproduction, and a struggle for food ensued, as did aggression.

The mighty first father god made a good order of the environment and life, while frail humans receive blame for causing disorder. Unwilling to shoulder complete blame for the disorder of existence, monotheistic authors later blamed a human-like enemy of the good god as the cause of disorder. In monotheistic speak, the personality names are of course Satan or the Devil.

Needing help to maintain order and to manage the disorder of life, and not finding a real helper, Jews, Christians, and Muslims, imagine a first father helper who cares for them as he made the first humans. For monotheists, in the beginning, a perfect order was made by a perfect first father god. Then came the first disorder into existence, portrayed as occurring between the first father god and the first two humans.

This scenario is patently a fiction as a perfect order has never existed and never will. Only in an artistically imagined story does a perfect beginning exist.

A human father who imposes family order, is the earthly model for an imagined first father god who imposes parental order on the family of humankind. The god of the biblical Genesis story ordered all things into existence and also ordered humans to obey commands for social order.

That which orders the environment into existence is simplistically imagined to be a first father word-using god. What orders the universe uses no words to do so. How does the environment move? It is a cosmological force that at every instant orders all relative motion of which environmental and living forms are a continuation. A nonlocal non-apparent force, not a parent voice of a human-like god, causes both order and disorder of the environment. The earth orders the functions of life, and for humans the subconscious animating triune soul orders the conscious self and vice versa.

Human conscious intelligence of the cerebral cortex of the brain does not come from a greater intelligence but from the lesser intelligence of the evolving cerebellum, midbrain, and body functions. These come from the non-intelligent yet order and disorder of the mother-like matrix of the earth and solar environment. The living offspring of the earth mimic the orderly and disorderly conduct of the environment.

Disorder

Only the Aryan prince Siddhartha Gautama, also known as Buddha (circa 623-543 BCE) of India has been truthful enough to declare life to be dukkha, usually translated to mean suffering or painful. A more accurate translation of the word dukkha is, ill-fit-together, and consists of parts.

This being so, means that the order of life is permeated with the potential to experience both biological and psychological disorder. Buddha also declared the Hindu gods to be mere metaphors; at least that is how he usually referred to them. The gods are artistic imaginings and so are ineffective at maintaining order and remedying the disorders of living.

According to tradition, after his insightful experience of nirvana at about thirty-five years of age, Buddha proceeded to live out his remaining life span by teaching others how to have a more orderly life. Buddha taught that this can be accomplished mainly through disciplines of meditation, acquiring insight, and practice of ethics. He avoided the disorder of society by forest dwelling or monastic living. He taught that the disorder of living can be reduced to maintain a manageable level of order. This is an existential task each individual must accomplish by their own efforts.

To reduce the disorder of daily living, an individual must reduce the internal disorder of the brain content of picture images and willing. Meditation relaxes and restores the body to a natural order and reduces the disorder of rampant picture images of the cerebral cortex of the brain. Yoga and physical exercise is the effort to reduce disorder and to strengthen the orderly function of the body.

The Greek word moira or fate is a felt order of human vulnerability to sequence and unrelenting causal time moving unerringly to a minimal alterable or unalterable disorderly outcome. In contrast, the relief of a sequence of disorder by a sudden restoration of order is often deemed an intervention and miracle performed by a first father god.

From the current of almighty time comes both order and the eroding twin of disorder. The continuing effort to obtain and maintain order succeeds for a time until disorder soon erodes all away. If successful in avoiding the disorders of serious illness and injury, an individual is swept along on the fast moving currents of life that all too soon flow more slowly to eventually enter into a peaceful bay of mild waves and relative calm.

An individual not attached to the things of life loved and utilized, and not overly encountering any uncaring opposition or aggression, sees the setting sun of the earthly dimension as it nears the hazy horizon, and arrives at numinous peace with what has been, is, and will be.

Construction

To shine the light of comprehension on the origin of existence has until quite recently been notoriously difficult to accomplish. In the Semitic past, the beginning was artistically described in words and stories. Jewish scribes eventually assembled the stories into a collection of books known as the Tanak. Christians glommed their own verbal artwork into the Bible. Muslims later followed with their collected verbal artwork of the Quran.

It is generally agreed that to do good is to assist fellow humans. Some humans assist others to comprehend the origin of existence by advocating the artistic verbal story of a monotheistic first father god. A first father is an artistic good for the greater portion of under-educated humankind as the god story serves to simplify and make plain the beginning of existence and also provides care and protection. Monotheistic religion is interested in what is subjectively good for humankind based on faith, belief, and tradition but is not overly interested in a demonstration of what is objectively true. This orientation is in stark contrast to the legal system of justice and science that both actively seek to reveal the good of objective facts.

A human-like origin is not a revelation from a god but is a self-revelation from the conscious cerebral cortex of the brain provoked by a strong subconscious need to comprehend the beginning of existence and to procure care and protection. The view that a human-like god exists is not a revealed truth from an objective higher intelligence outside the human brain but is an artistic subjective truth constructed by the cerebral cortex.

The conscious self, the cerebral cortex of the brain, constructs a first father god as a way of denoting the origin of existence. Yet the life of the human body is not constructed by a god. Life is constructed by a soul, an animating triune forcible hunger for food, sex and reproduction, and aggression. The animating soul as a triune force is a continuation of the energy elements of the environment, and the unseen surround of a cosmological force that ever exists on its own.

Human origin as a first father god is the limiting way the cerebral cortex of the brain constructs a beginning. It is the human brain and a limited and dim comprehension that confines human origin to a first forefather in a long genealogical line of previous earthly fathers.

Monotheism, the folk view that there exists a human-like first father god of all fathers, began in the Semitic Middle East and later spread to Europe and Western culture. The view of a first father god is the traditional but erroneous way the cerebral cortex of the brain reveals human origin. The first father is not merely a glorious forefather but by making the greater vast environment, is also glorified to be a powerful god that exceeds mere forefather status.

Polytheism, the view there are many gods and goddesses is subjectively true but they do not exist objectively. The deities exist only as artistic products of imagination that serve to explain to humans the nonhuman cause and effect function of the environment and life. Modern monotheism denies the existence of other gods in an effort to trump them and to universalize a shared beginning of humans. Monotheism insists on the untruthful subjective delusion that a first father god objectively exists.

Truth is better served by observation and comprehension of how the cerebral cortex of the brain constructs its own origin. The purported wisdom of a first father god, or the written words of monotheism, pale in comparison to a wise human observer of the human condition and brain and body functions.

Monotheistic utterances by and about a first father god are an infectious cloudy sputum of vague imaginations that obscure healthy clear human comprehension. Monotheistic writings are a testament not to objective truth but to subjective artistic imagination that portrays the beginning of existence to be a caring first father god. For those who care to closely examine, the function of life always mutely testifies that it is a continuation of the earth environment and not from a first father god.

Only in subjective imagination does a first father god exist to care for humans. It is the real subconscious soul that forcibly cares for life by a hunger for food, sex and reproduction, and aggression. The triune soul cares about getting and eating food, having sex and reproduction, and expressing aggression, and so cares for each individual life.

Care

Beginning with conception, progressing through fetal development, and continuing on from birth into childhood and through adulthood, human life consists of many cares. Family members seek to both receive care and to give care, and cooperate with each other to obtain care. Coworkers care to cooperate with fellow employees yet usually care more for the job than each other. Strangers usually display a basic level of human care toward each other.

Life is composed of verb and noun parts, and much individual effort is required to care for and to keep various parts in working order that continuously change. A great deal of a lifetime consists of working to care for and to maintain physical and mental order and to avoid disorder. Human life often has to struggle to survive and flounder for safety, health, knowledge, relationships, and money.

Finding the environment, other animal species, and fellow humans to be mostly uncaring, Semitic humans began to imagine a caring first father god. Many modern humans continue to subjectively imagine a first father god that cares for them.

Realistically, it is only the non-caring environment that both supports and does not support the life it brings forth and receives at the time of death.

Theology is the inappropriate use of reason to investigate and to advocate for what is the artistic imagining of a monotheistic first father god. A first father is a subjective cognitive mooring of safety, an imaginative anchor to avoid drifting on the vicissitudes of life, the strong tides and tossing waves of real daily living. A first father god is but the furthermost imagined terminus of the evolved sexual reproduction of a long line of biological fathers.

Many theologians, scholars, and lay persons debate the truth contained in the writings of monotheistic religions. What a foolish waste of time and human effort. Theology is art, a subjective imagining and elaborating of a first father god. The supposed reliable knowledge of a human-like god is but a subjective imagining of the beginning of the environment and life to be a first father. This is a dead end, a blind alley, an error of artistic imagination and superficial tradition mistaken to be objectively reasoned and real knowledge. Instead of clearly observing life to be a continuation of the environment, a monotheistic first father god is imagined to exist.

If a god is not represented visually in sculpture or painting, then it is presented as a verbal work of art in story form. For some time the artistic fictional works of the Bible, Quran, and other monotheistic writings have attracted attention from the public. Too bad for those who follow the impaired intellectual tradition of theology, as each stares and strains not with objective truth but with subjective works of art. Theistic writings about a human-like god are a mere artistic literary expression of human concern about themselves.

Humankind must and will eventually cease to pay attention to the empty words and rituals of monotheistic religion and its first father god. It will eventually be accepted that a monotheistic god is but a simplistic story that renders an artistic beginning of existence. Ever the universe goes on its way without a single word. This is in stark contrast to the many wasted words of monotheistic writings.

Beginning

Imagining an ancestor first father god, is an attempt to remove ignorance of the beginning. The "word of God" as the bible is often referred to, are words produced by the human cerebral cortex of the brain that writes an imagined artistic story of a first father beginning. Most astoundingly, through ignorance and popular tradition, theistic subjective artistic stories have been accepted as objectively true.

The human attempt of finding refuge from the environment and life by identifying the beginning to be a human-like god, occurs solely in subjective artistic imagination and is mistaken by many, educated and uneducated, for what is true. For many, just the thought of a first father god provides a satisfactory answer to the question of where everything comes from. The god also provides a higher authority figure of care and protection. A first father god is a way of transcending what came after the origin of existence, the environment and then life. What made higher human life must by necessity for human comprehension, be identified as a first glorified human forefather, a god.

A much better orientation to transcending ignorance of the beginning is meditation practice. A meditation practice disciplines conscious attention to focus and observe a reality of sensations of the senses, and the derived conscious picture images of the cerebral cortex of the brain. Then can then be better observed the subjective mental making of artificial gods as an imaginary artistic explanation for the beginning and events of existence.

Fixing or focusing attention during meditation reduces an over-abundance of conscious picture images of the cerebral cortex of the brain. Then can be better observed the subconscious function of the body as a forcible hunger for food, sex and reproduction, and aggression. This dynamic, it can be declared, is the animating triune soul that can be aesthetically sensed or intuited to be a continuation of the energy elements of the earth.

The animating impetus of life and what activates the motion of the earth, solar system, galaxy, and the universe cannot be observed directly but can be inferred to be a cosmological force that ever exists on its own. A cosmological force is the real animator of an existence of relative motion of the environment and living forms.

For preliterate, prescientific, and modern under-educated and unscientific persons, the animating of life is imagined to be a noun animator parent, a first father god. A true animate, is not an ancestor first mate imagined to be a human-like father and glorified to be a greater god. The true animator of life is the supportive matrix of the earth and a continuation of it as an animating triune soul, a dynamic forcible bodily hunger for food, sex and reproduction, and aggression.

The internal animation of life can be traced to the external supportive energy of the earth, and inferred to be a continuation of the greater motion of the universe. A cosmological force cannot be measured, only inferred from the combined relative motion of the universe, the environment, and life. The visible universe is a continuation of a nonvisible ground, a sole cosmological force that ever exists on its own.

The animating of life is a real forcible hunger for food, sex and reproduction, and aggression. The next real presence is that of the supportive earth. Achieving the clarity of nirvana, Siddhartha Gautama, later known as the Buddha (circa 623-543 BCE) touched the real earth as a witness to his accomplishment of awakening. The Buddha utilized his own real efforts to comprehend and therefore he did not acknowledge or utter thanks to an imaginary beginning, a human-like first father god. Instead, he recognized the cause and effect of karma proceeding and evolving through lifetimes.

The Buddha touched the earth immediately upon his awakening. This act is usually interpreted to mean that the earth served as an anthropomorphic witness to his accomplishment. A more realistic interpretation is that Buddha recognized the support of the earth in his quest.

Buddha did not reach out to touch an imagined human-like god for his enlightenment but touched what is most akin to his life and to all life, the very real supportive earth.

Inside Job

The monotheistic view of life is that it is an outside job, made by a first father god. In reality life is an inside job, as supported by an outside earth environment. Life is a continuation of what is immediately outside of it, the environment, and further outside of the earth, life is a continuation of a cosmological force.

An imaginary benevolent monotheistic first father god masquerades for the real supportive earth and an animating triune human soul of a forcible hunger for food, sex and reproduction, and aggression. Sad but true, the nonobservant and nonscientific monotheistic religions overlook the inside animating soul of life and instead settle on the explanation of a first father god to be the origin of existence. Jewish literary artists began the fantastic view that in a past time a first father god made life without a soul, and that for humans at least, the body has to be physically remade or resurrected in a future time. The religion of Judaism neglects the inside animating soul for an outside first father god.

Dissociation

According to the Diagnostic and Statistical Manual of Mental Disorders (DSM) a dissociation disorder is often precipitated by stress, trauma, or drugs. Dissociation is a psychological defense or coping mechanism, a way of detaching from reality as a response to reduce boredom, conflict, or pain. The disorder ranges along a spectrum from mild daydreaming, altered states of extrasensory perception, and to severe disorientation and emotional depersonalization and amnesia.

Dissociation is a psychological way of detaching from the reality of immediate surroundings of the environment.

A monotheistic human-like god is a psychological dissociation disorder. An imagined first father is how many humans separate themselves from the environment, from other life forms, and from lower level humans of the less intelligent and less well behaved variety. For many average people the only way to identify the origin of existence is to imagine it to be a first father, and since he made all things, he is thought of as a god. A dissociation from the earth occurs when a simplistic human ideational effort imagines the beginning of the environment and life to be a first father god.

Ask

For some monotheists, to accept that the human species was made or created by a god in the beginning is not enough. Christians have the audacious view that the Semitic god actually begot a male child with a human female. The verses of Luke 11:9 and Matthew 7:7 portray Jesus, the supposed son of a first father god and the founder of the Christian religion, as saying:

"Ask, and it shall be given you; seek, and ye shall find; knock and it shall be opened unto you."

A more realistic version of the verse might be the following words: "Ask and it may or may not be given to you; seek and you might or might not find; knock and the door may not be opened, or might be opened to you if someone is home."

There is no first father god beginning at home in the universe to respond to the knocking prayers of humans. The obsessive petitioning prayer to a first father is a comforting delusion, a mistaken idea. To go too far by insisting on being given something, finding something, or a door being opened may result in a psychological obsessional disorder.

The only real response to asking, seeking, and knocking, is from a cosmological force and a cause and effect sequence of energy that imbues the universe.

A first father god is a mere imaginary subjective metaphor; it does not exist objectively. The only dwelling place of a first father god is in the cerebral cortex of the human brain. Cause and effect sequence measures, makes, and rules both the order and disorder of a many dimensional universe.

Jesus

In the gospel of Matthew, Jesus is portrayed as uttering the follow words:

"Therefore whosoever hearth these sayings of mine and doeth them, I will liken him unto a wise man, which built his house upon a rock: And the rain descended, and the floods came, and the winds blew, and beat upon that house; and it fell not: for it was founded upon a rock. And everyone that heareth these sayings of mine, and doeth them not, shall be likened unto a foolish man, which built his house upon the sand: and the rain descended, and the floods came, and the winds blew, and beat upon that house; and it fell: and great was the fall of it." (Matthew 7:24-26)

In the gospel of Matthew Jesus is asked a question to which he replies:

"Master, which is the greatest commandment in the law? Jesus said unto him, Thou shalt love the Lord thy God with all thy heart, and with all thy soul, and with all thy mind. This is the first and great commandment. And the second is like unto it, Thou shalt love thy neighbor as thyself. On these two commandments hang all the law and the prophets." (Matthew 22:36-40)

While Jesus taught using numerous parables and sayings, the mention of the two commandments are considered by many to be the bedrock of his teachings. The two commandments are considered by Jesus to be the basis of all commandments and contain in essence the teachings of the prophets.

The teachings of Jesus are to love the origin of existence as a first father god, and to love neighbors as oneself. These two commandments are intended to serve as truths upon which to build a strong foundation of life.

Most humans work hard to build a sound footing of support upon which to build their individual lives. Humans work to obtain an education so as to enter into a career and to obtain financial success. Yet life is built on the shifting sands of time and change of the environment and the physical body. Conscious life is also built on the ever shifting subconscious animating triune soul.

To love a shared human origin is to love only an imaginary metaphor intended to give subjective but not objective stability. A first father god is a product not of science or mathematics but is derived as an artistic imaginary way of identifying an unknown beginning of existence.

The bedrock teaching to love your neighbor as yourself is fraught with peril. The conscious self of each individual is an uneven match for the subconscious animating soul. The conscious self is doomed to be supported by the subconscious triune soul, an essence of a forcible hunger for food, sex and reproduction, and aggression.

Few individuals can genuinely like, care for and love another person. The essence of individuality is the subconscious soul, a triune forcible hunger for food, sex and reproduction, and aggression. How can someone really love this agglomeration in others? Both the outside environment and the inside soul forcibly trouble individual conscious reasoning.

The god Yhwh commanded the Jews to love a neighbor just as an individual loves his own life. (Leviticus 19: 13-17) Jesus later commanded this as well "Thou shalt love thy neighbor as thyself." (Mark 12:31, Matthew 22:39) It is much easier to love the conscious self of our neighbor but this command does not realistically take into account the brutish subconscious soul.

The individual human soul is the animating function of the body. The biological body is vulnerable to disease, injury, ageing, and dying. Therefore, it is not easy to really care for and to love the soul and the body of others.

It is easier to love the conscious self, the cerebral cortex of others as it alone is capable of reasoning. It is an almost impossible feat, even for a bona fide saint to love a neighbor's subconscious triune soul, a narrow and egocentric interest of caring for individual survival as a forcible hunger for food, sex and reproduction, and aggression.

Vaunted romantic and sexual love, and family, friendship, and companionate love, easily transform into the aggression of possessiveness, jealously, envy, and verbal and physical aggression. Relationships generate an ambivalent conflict between the conscious self of the cerebral cortex, and the subconscious of the cerebellum, midbrain and body. The body is a lesser conscious function of an animating triune soul, a forcible hunger for food, sex and reproduction, and aggression.

The sentiment of Jesus (Mark 12:31) who asks his fellow humans to love imperfect neighbors as our self, must also be broadened to include at least some species of animals and plants, and the environment.

Punishment

Since the monotheistic first father god is said to be perfect and Mary the mother of Jesus is deemed to be born without original sin, then the procreated son must also be perfect. The perfect Jesus is then portrayed as dying for the imperfections of other humans. According to Christian theology, Jesus died as a substitute for humans. This substitute is said to avert the wrath and punishment of a first father god toward humans for their evil deeds.

Life is often a punishing experience but there is no punisher. The dynamic punishing of life is limited knowledge, and the triune soul of a forcible hunger for food, sex and reproduction, and aggression.

Eating excess or unhealthy food punishes the eater. Sex is the begetting of life and the punishment of caring for and protecting it from the many harmful experiences of living. Verbal and physical aggression are punishing to both the perpetrator and the victim.

The subjective conception of a first father god originating in the cerebral cortex of the brain blurs and distorts reality. Life is not a punishment by a first father god artistically imagined by monotheistic religions but as a continuation of the changing environment, is clearly a malfunction of parts.

So declared the clear sighted and awakened Buddha (circa 623-543 BCE) that life is dukkha, meaning suffering as it is composed of parts. What the monotheistic religions imagine as the punishments of a first father god, Buddha sanely saw as dukkha, the suffering of the changing conditions of not enough or too much for the fluctuating parts of life.

First Father

A first father god is a cognitive response of imagining by the cerebral cortex of the brain as a way of identifying an unknown beginning. The beginning is portrayed in story as a special event for humans. Yet humans are no more special than are other living forms including bacteria and viruses. A human-like god is only a human way of portraying the beginning of existence.

Wanting to have personal experience of a first father god is really an attempt to be less dominated by the less conscious and subconscious forcible triune soul. The goal then is to have the more conscious reasoning and intelligent cerebral cortex of the brain predominate and so to better build on and acquire knowledge, strength, and possessions. An imagined knowledgeable first father also stimulates humans to emulate and be more godlike by acquiring more knowledge and by emulating the good god through ethical behavior.

Imagining a first father god is a human way of wanting to survive life and death. A human-like god is an imaginary way of having a greater intelligence to comprehend events of the environment and life. The expended effort to search for, to contact, and to have personal experience of a first father intelligent god is the individual human effort to increase comprehension of the cerebral cortex of the brain. The only way to reach a better comprehension of reality is by reducing the real confusion of excess picture images, and to reduce the animating triune soul of forcible hunger for food, sex and reproduction, and aggression.

To seek a better comprehension of reality by seeking a first father god is to rely on what is strictly artistic and imaginary. The mere idea of a first father god quickly allies an individual with an imaginary intelligent and special beginning. Orienting to a past time of a first father maker, bolsters individual importance in the often unimportant times of daily life.

Concoction

There is a story of a Greek philosopher who when speaking to a crowd assembled, they abruptly began to applaud him. Perplexed and curious, the philosopher then turned to his companion and asked, "Did I just say something foolish?" Similarly today, the human crowd loudly and foolishly applauds the existence of a first father god.

In reality, a monotheistic god is an artistic and artificial subjective concoction, foolishly and unthinkingly accepted and applauded by the modern crowd to be objectively real. The concoction consists of multiple ingredients or needs, an existential desire to know the beginning of existence, a need for care and protection, how to live on earth, and what happens after physical death.

A monotheistic first father god is an artistic creative way of imagining the beginning of existence. A monotheistic god is a concocted medication, a subjective medication to make an individual feel better in the all too brief struggle of life.

Fear of the unknown is reduced and tranquilized by identifying the origin of existence to be a caring and protective first father god. A father of all fathers is a subjectively imagined and concocted medication.

If what makes all things does so with intention, such as a first father god, then the intention can be changed to direct events for the better and not for the worse. It is the cerebral cortex of the brain that conceives of and values the beginning of existence to be intentional and to be good. The only real intention is that of humans who concoct a poor and fantastic solution to identify the beginning of existence and to procure care and protection.

To appeal to an external higher first father god is in reality an appeal to what is higher internally, the cerebral cortex of the human brain that can comprehend more about reality and how to treat other humans better. A first father god is a subjective idea not an objective reality. This is why there are so many gods with subjectively differing attributes in various cultures. For monotheistic religions, the god is human-like, male, and is not visible. The god is presented as a first father figure from which the generations of human fathers come from.

For monotheistic Jews, Christians, and Muslims, the animating of life is not a soul but is accomplished only from the outside by an animator, a first father maker god. The god then has the future task of reanimating, remaking, or resurrecting and saving the bodily lives of his monotheistic offspring. The simplistic view of a monotheistic first father god ignores the animating soul of life and how it is a continuation of the energy elements of the earth that is in turn a continuation of a cosmological force that ever exists on its own.

Buddy System

A monotheistic god is a distorting influence on cognitive clarity and is a lazy unthinking shortcut to know the beginning of existence.

Monotheism is an individual and group psychological delusion that is most difficult to remedy. Only much time and study can reduce the long term psychological delusion of humankind that seeks to live life based on an imaginary buddy system. A buddy system is defined as:

"A cooperative practice of pairing two or more people together for mutual assistance or safety."

Monotheism is the practice whereby humans imagine and pair themselves with a first father god who can assist them and contribute to personal safety. The buddy system is set up in the human cerebral cortex of the brain exclusively for human benefit. The monotheistic buddy system is one-sided as there is not much humans can do for the god except to be good to each other rather than evil. Yet to be good for approval or to receive a reward from someone for goodness, is to not be genuinely good. Doing what is good is its own reward of feeling good.

A monotheistic first father god is a subjective make-believe process, an artistic imagining and then believing. For those who accept that a first father god objectively exists, the monotheistic nonvisible buddy continually accompanies and protects an individual. To turn to an ostensible objective first father god is in reality a subjective resorting to the cerebral cortex of the human brain. To be more god-like translates to being more like the reasoning cerebral cortex of the brain.

Based on memory and verbal and written stories of previous generations, there is imagined a story of a first father. Creative artistic imagination portrays the beginning of existence to be made by a first father god. For the primitive cerebral cortex of the Semitic brain, the beginning of humans could not be portrayed otherwise.

The often desperate focus of attention on the artistic word portrait of a first father, has through time caused a cognitive fixation that continues into modern times as evidenced by the widespread notion of a universal god.

Monotheistic scriptures are subjective, artistic, imagined stories portrayed as objectively real. Reaching out in thought and emotion to a first father god brings relief and comfort to many. Yet this psychological process, however long based as a tradition, is a desperate delusion.

Monotheistic religion is an immature and false way of reconnecting to the beginning of the environment and life. The true way of reconnecting is to observe and comprehend that the function of brain and body is a continuation of the supportive earth environment, and further is a continuation of a transcendent cosmological force that moves all things into, through and out of existence.

Knowing

It is often difficult to learn and to increase individual intelligence. It is easier just to imagine and believe there is a greater intelligence that knows everything of past, present, and future. It is ironic that a first father god subjectively represents higher human knowledge yet is objectively false.

Life is a chore that consists of a sequence and series of chores. The traditional way of getting to know a first father god is to live a secluded or monastic lifestyle away from the behaviors and knowing of daily social life. Also practiced are fasting and regulating of food, celibacy, and non-aggression. These are ways of increasing human comprehension of the conscious functions of the cerebral cortex of the brain, and simultaneously of subduing and balancing a subconscious soul.

When monotheistic religion founders and leaders claim to experience or get nearer to a first father god, they are in reality experiencing an elevated ability of the cerebral cortex of the brain. Insight, intuition, creativity, inventiveness, and extra-sensory perception are examples.

To get closer to a first father god is to develop higher or better human perception, reasoning, and comprehension. Ascending to a god is in reality raising human awareness to a higher functioning level of the cerebral cortex of the brain. Doing so simultaneously subdues the animating triune soul of hunger for food, sex and reproduction, and aggression.

There are two main types of knowing, a conscious cerebral cortex knowing and consequent behaviors, and a subconscious midbrain and body knowing and behaviors. The conscious cerebral cortex imagines a human-like god and reasons, while the subconscious midbrain furnishes intuitions, dreams, and regulates the body. Both systems function differently yet must complement each other for holistic function.

Monotheistic religion is all about an imagined first father god, pragmatically utilized to ameliorate the real struggle of life and a real animating triune soul. The good of the evolved cerebral cortex is its higher ability to reason and the lesser good of imagining a first father god. The imagined conscious god counters the risk of an uncertain nonconscious environment, and the internal subconscious animating triune soul of the body replete with its many potential and active evil behaviors of hunger for food, sex and reproduction, and aggression. To rally to a first father god is a call to better utilize the cerebral cortex of the brain.

The minor part of the human brain is the sixteen billion conscious reasoning neurons of the cerebral cortex. The major part of humans is the subconscious seventy billion neurons of the cerebellum and midbrain, and the ten trillion cells of plexuses, autonomic nervous system, and organs of the body that are not rational or capable of reasoning. Therefore humans lack sufficient reason and tend to lean much more toward irrationality and even craziness. Humans are crazy for foods, for sex or its reproductive results, and crazy for aggression as physical and verbal behaviors, and its more benign expressions of competition sports and games.

The animating triune soul is a forcible hunger for food, sex and reproduction, and aggression. Therefore, the essence of human life is to eat, fuck, and fight. Most other activities are extraneous and even unnecessary.

Life

The truth demonstrated by founders of religions is that humans have the capacity to care for and act in a healing way toward others. Yet the effort by individuals to realize this better potential is often discarded to instead favor abusing, harming, and killing of fellow humans.

Worse than the poignant waste and loss of human potential for the better in life, is the confounding of life with an emphasis on a false metaphor by monotheistic religions. A human-like first father god is substituted for the truth of a genealogical line of sexual reproduction by biological fathers that only occurs supported by the earth. The triune soul grows and evolves life that is a continuation of and is supported by the energy elements of the earth and solar environments.

A first father god hovers over humans only in imagination to explain the beginning of existence and to provide imaginary care and protection. The subjectively imagined fatherly god is an ersatz explanation for the beginning of existence. A monotheistic imagined god fails to care for and protect his humans, and the rampant sufferings of daily life continue unabated.

Prayers directed to a first father god, are really intended for the intelligent cerebral cortex of the brain. Directing attention to a first father god is the intention to expand and elevate human comprehension, especially knowledge of the beginning of existence. Yet directing attention to a first father god is a primitive and a persistently continuing modern delusion. Sexual reproduction by many forebears and evolution supported by the earth environment is the only true origin of life.

Life consists mainly of continuing daily efforts to experience pleasures and to avoid numerous pains. Directing attention to a first father god is an ideational pleasure and at least furnishes imaginary relief from discomfort and pain.

Observing reality, humans have to direct attention and exert effort to obtain pleasures so as to continue living and to make life worthwhile. Humans direct attention to obtaining the pleasure of eating food that temporarily reduces the pains of hunger, and to find a sexual partner for the pleasures of sex and reproduction that alleviate the pains of physical frustration. Aggression is temporarily pleasurable when the expression of it relieves or removes limitation, frustration, and threat.

Life is difficult. It is difficult to maintain physical and psychological health, difficult to learn much, and difficult to work and make money. It is difficult to maintain relationships. Life mainly revolves around behaviors of obtaining food, genital pleasure and reproduction, and aggression. It is difficult to build lasting happiness on the changing and fleeting pleasures of eating food, sex and reproduction, and aggression.

Yet no matter how disappointing and wretched, most seek to prolong and to have life. The aim of life is to have more pleasures and less pains, yet the many players lose and few win the game of life. Eventually each, young or old, partially or fully awaken to the many possible or actual hazards and dangers of living. Looking at many others who fail at the endeavor and tasks of daily living, each may shudder and express silent thankfulness for individual skill, luck, or being favored by a first father god for avoidance of the difficult path of failure taken by so many.

Each individual is tasked with bringing quality experience to their own life and to that of others. Since the quality of life for many is so poor and difficult, then the mirage of a first father god is much appreciated and willingly imagined to be real.

Young and Old

Both children and adults receive woefully insufficient education in the important areas of life. The main areas of importance are:

Health
Knowledge
Money
Relationships

In the language of India, there is avidya or ignorance about life. In monotheistic speak, there is sin, a separation from higher knowledge of life as artistically portrayed by a human-like god.

Many young and old ignore the importance of keeping fit. Many are separate from the higher knowledge of keeping physically and mentally fit. Supportive evidence for this assertion is that many do not exert adequate effort to keep fit through exercise and diet. The companies that purvey fast food, soda, candy, and their advertising, lure both young and adults into unhealthy lifestyles. No human-like first father god will ever intervene to promote health.

Many ignore the importance of learning in life and are thus separate from an adequate higher level of knowledge. Many fail to learn about the environment and living forms. Many fail in acquiring adequate knowledge, especially of the human brain and body. The practice of meditation and knowledge of the distinction between the conscious self and subconscious soul should be made mandatory and compulsory.

Too many ignore the importance of earning in life and are thus separate from an adequate higher level knowledge of financial wealth. Little is taught in grade schools, middle, and high schools about the importance of acquiring skills of how to earn, save, and invest money.

Far too many ignore the importance of relationships in life and are thus separate from an adequate higher level knowledge of the dynamics of successful and fulfilling relationships.

Scant knowledge is communicated in grade, middle, and high schools on how to develop and maintain the quality of personal relationships of family, friends, and coworkers. It should be clearly taught that relationships are like medicines, they both help and harm.

While young, each individual must exert the effort to remove ignorance and to be successful in acquiring higher knowledge of health and fitness. The wise keep fit, learn much, earn much, and cultivate supportive relationships.

Musings on Life and Death

Advice to the young, to see fellow humans clearly, always see them in their true light as inherently bad and evil, and only then look for any convincing evidence of some small good in them. Realizing the bad to be primary in a person, only then look for any secondary good.

Based on daily experience of the low worth of existence, a first father god is imagined who can repair the sad condition of human life. Yet, the only real worth of life exists as ephemeral pleasures and recurring efforts to satisfy a recurrent hunger for food, needs for sex and reproduction, and aggression.

Humans observe how fleeting and often uncertain life is. Life is fragile, vulnerable, easily harmed, and frequently misled. There is observed little that is long-lasting in life and its demise and decay is apparent daily. Observing that all on earth sooner or later passes away with time, humans easily become melancholy.

Then what is held to be of value is questioned. Doubt, skepticism and pessimism arise to cast a pallor over existence and to devalue or at least dull even the good times of life. The fact of death immediately makes life only half worth living. Death spoils the worth of life. The struggle of painful physical and psychological experiences further reduce and lower the worth of life.

From this awareness surely comes the "I don't care" attitude of cruelty and crime and a vast spectrum of ethical and moral infractions and failures.

Sleep resembles and subtly reminds of the evidential fact of future biological death. Ethereal dreams are a nightly reminder of a future afterlife dimension. The supporting evidence for the existence of an afterlife includes anecdotal reports and research into near-death experiences, extrasensory perception that transcends physical senses, childhood remembrances of past lives, and anecdotal reports by relatives and friends of sensing deceased persons. These experiences combine to lend credence and gently push the possibility of an afterlife existence into the status realm of at least probability if not fact.

Lack of knowledge aggravates both life and a potential afterlife, and the fixing of stupid remains ever an individual burden of effort. Lacking comprehension, many succumb to the pathologies of daily living. When someone dies with whom there is a bond of care and love, the experience draws an individual away from living, more toward better seeing the equal advantages of both life and death.

Valuable Knowledge

To identify the beginning of existence is a valuable knowledge. Those who claim to have knowledge of the origin of existence, certainly have a big advantage over those who do not. In lieu of actual observational scientific evidence or mathematically measured knowledge, only by utilizing artistic imagination to craft stories can primitive knowledge of a beginning be exclaimed.

Monotheistic writings primitively exclaim that the beginning of existence is a first father god. In the biblical Garden of Eden story, everything that exists of the environment and life was made and provided by a first father god. The first humans were endowed with a basic level of intelligence but obtained some of the god's own knowledge he had deposited in a special Tree of Knowledge of Good and Evil.

The humans proceeded to oppose the god, utilizing the god's very own knowledge. Eating the special fruit increased basic endowed human knowledge, and also stimulated and awakened the dormant sexual organs the god had created for the first two humans.

In tribal and folk thinking, something somewhere must have a higher knowledge of how life is made. Since the environment and life is so intricate and difficult for humans to comprehend, there must exist a very intelligent forefather, glorified to be a god. The story of a first father is the artistic way for limited human intelligence to increase knowledge by imagining the beginning to be a super father.

The use of visual and verbal art long preceded mathematics and science. Those prone to monotheistic thinking, artistically imagine a first father that began a long genealogical line and sequence of biological fathers. If there is a numerical sequence of fathers then the error of thinking is there must be a first father of all later fathers. The first father has to and must be a special and super father, a god.

The identifying of an unknown beginning to be a first father god is accomplished through artistic imagination and story. Monotheism is not empirical nor is it a system of mathematics. Monotheism, the view there is a first father god, is an artistic imaginative use of story images to go back in time to a human-like beginning.

The beginning of the environment and life must be simple enough for the under-educated and average person to comprehend. In modern times, knowledge acquired by the average person is limited to secondary schooling, family, peers, and media of internet, television, movies, magazines, and newspapers. The average person therefore fails to adequately explore the topic of monotheism.

A first father god is created by directing attention back in time past many biological fathers to a completely imagined first father. This primitive way of thinking by Semitic storytellers of a first father, has in modern times been normalized and accepted to be reliable knowledge.

A true story told to descendants about previous fathers and grandfathers is extended by creative imagination to be an entirely untrue story of a special first father, a progenitor of progeny. A first father god is merely a distorted memory of many biological forefathers condensed into an imagined and glorified first father.

Unreasonable Folk

It is the nonreasoning environment and the poor reasoning of humans that cause some to imagine a reasonable first father god. Over time the god is then accepted by many to be real. Monotheism is a folk religion of the under-educated masses. A first father imagined and superimposed over the universe provides a poor primitive folk answer to the question of how the environment and life came to exist.

Not a reasonable first father god but the unreasonable environment and individual conscious and subconscious unreasoning choices direct each person to their destination. For many this comprehension and responsibility is unbearable. Therefore, monotheism, the view there is only one first father god, is accepted and practiced by Judaism, Christianity, and Islam, and by humans in general. Monotheism is a folk view of reality. The word folk is defined as:

"The common people of a country or society who represent a traditional way of life as practiced in the arts, customs, and religious beliefs and rituals that constitute a distinctive culture."

The folk imagine a lot but reason little. It is the common folk who keep the custom of artistically imagining a first father god going through many years. Religious rituals are an unthinking folk way of promoting social order by imitation, as all attending do the same repeated behavior during a religious service. Performing the orderly and best behaviors in the presence of an imagined authority as a first father god, also contributes to the social order of the human family gathering.

For average folks the beginning is simplistically and easily comprehended when told it is a first father god. The folk religions of monotheism are based on the unthinking acceptance of common people living in the Middle East and Western societies.

Monotheism is based on artistic imagination of a first father god to explain the beginning of the environment and life, and to obtain care and protection. Monotheistic writings are not based on revelations from a first father god to humans. Monotheistic writings and the entire field of theology are based entirely on human imagining of the cerebral cortex of the brain.

When subjective monotheistic imaginings are accepted as reliable and true, they can then be psychologically diagnosed and classified as delusions and mistaken folk ideas. Monotheism impairs, distorts, and mars clear perception of life to be a real continuation of the earth environment, and all relative motion of the universe to be a continuation of a cosmological force, field, or ground that ever exists on its own.

Imagined Beginning

Life is limited by the environment, and limited by time to change, age, and die. Life is limited by biology to hunger for food, to have sex and reproduction, and to be aggressive. The poignant human experience of limitation cannot be undone in a rapid, practical, inventive, and physical way.

Having the evolved ability to imagine, the human cerebral cortex of the brain can quickly change life for the better by imagining a first father god and artistically portraying it in story. The imagining of a first father is a way of leaving now limitations of knowledge for an artistic knowing of the beginning of existence. An imagined first father is also a way to receive imaginary care and protection in life, and if good, to look forward to the reward of an afterlife.

The beginning made by a first father god was not ever observed nor was it remembered.

Therefore, the beginning can only be imagined to be a first father as the beginning sequence of biological fathers, and mothers. The biblical Genesis version of the beginning of the environment and life is artistically fashioned with words and story.

An unknown beginning is made known through creative imagination and story. Humans observe plays, movies, television, and read fiction books, and in so doing often react emotionally by being frightened, moved to tears, or anger. Humans react to fiction characters and situations just as intensely as they do to what is real. It is often difficult to differentiate between what is imagined and imitated, and what is real.

A story is based on imagining whereas reasoning is supported by evidential observation and measuring. In the practice of law, reasoning is utilized to question and cross examine verbal and written statements. To imagine a beginning and to portray it in story as real is the simple farce of monotheism.

The conscious self, the cerebral cortex of the brain and central nervous system, has evolved the human ability for science and mathematics. Yet prior to these accomplishments, there evolved the earlier artistic ability to imagine various gods and goddesses, and also to imagine a first father god of monotheism.

Usually what is first is better than what is secondary. Therefore, a first father must be better than all later inferior fathers of succession. The notion of a first father is but a myth speculated on through the mists of times past and elaborated on by mere artistic imagination and spun into existence with words.

For early biblical peoples, it was not possible to observe or measure the origin of the universe. A nonscientific, nonmathematical, and nonobjective way of identifying the origin of existence had to be utilized. The only possible way to represent the beginning of existence was to artistically imagine it to be a first father god of many biological fathers.

The notion of a first father was further elaborated on with words and portrayed in story as true and real. However, the words about a first father god are objectively false and the story is a subjective and artistic fiction.

Imagining

The human brain is not able to observe a god through sensory sensations, or objectively reason about it as an observed object, or to measure it using mathematics. The human brain mistakes the idea of a first father god to be a result of reasoning when in reality it is a product of subjective imagining, a way of making an unknown beginning to be known.

To deny a first father god equates to denying one's own biological ancestry and genealogical heritage as this is what the monotheistic god represents. This is in great part why the imagined concept continues to endure in popular thinking.

A first dad of humans is imagined and utilized to provide protection and to help in choosing what is good and to avoid what is evil or bad in any known and unknown situations of life and death. Everyone needs help at some time in life. If real human help is lax or not available, then imagining a first father god who cared to make humans is implored to assist. The idea of a first father god is taught to those who are not proficient in reason and are most susceptible to imagination, the young and under-educated of society.

The inspiring yet artistic idea of a monotheistic god originated in Semitic thinking and over the years has been accepted by European and Western cultures. These advanced cultures fail miserably to comprehend that a first father god is a cultural tradition based on artistic imagination and story.

A monotheistic god is a way of focusing attention on the beginning of the environment and life.

A first father god is how the human cerebral cortex localizes and locates the origin of existence in a seeming infinite space and time by a leap of imagination from now to a past human-like beginning. Today it is known this leap of artistic imagination vaults over the real evidence of an origin and evolution from the earth. Referring to a monotheistic god in reality refers to the cerebral cortex of the brain where the god is subjectively imagined to exist objectively, as a first father cause of the environment and life.

A first father god is only an imagined good but the small number of sixteen billion neurons of the cerebral cortex of the brain is a real and valuable good that humans possess and that can both imagine and reason. Artistic imagination results in monotheistic religion and reasoning results in science

Faulty

Imagining a first father god to exist, is a faulty way of identifying the animator of life. In reality, the animator of life is the earth and solar environment. As a continuation of the elements of earth energy, the animating of life is a triune soul that forces life to live as a forcible hunger for food, sex and reproduction, and aggression. Both the animating triune soul and energy elements of the environment are dependent continuations of a cosmological force that continually and visibly moves the visible and nonvisible universe.

Many sense a connection and continuation from an unseen source to the relative forms of what is seen. Lacking the cognitive ability to discern a greater cosmological force that moves the universe, the imagined knowledge and label of a forefather god is applied to the origin of existence. The notion of a first father origin is a fiction. The monotheistic story of a first father beginning is mere human imagination grappling with an unknown beginning of existence. Humans attend monotheistic religious services as they seek to approach what is higher outside of themselves, accepted by attendees to be a first father god.

In reality, it is the higher function of the cerebral cortex of the brain that elevates human attention by imagining a first father god who is further identified as existent, and prior to the beginning of the environment and life.

Monotheism is an early subjective and artistic imaginative theory of the beginning. The theory has sufficed prior to the reduction of subjective thinking by insisting on objective scientific observation and mathematical measurement. Prior to the measuring and reasoning of science, the most prevalent way to know the beginning of existence was to imagine it in story as an artistic expression.

The cerebral cortex of the human brain makes a picture image story of the beginning of existence. The word story consists of imagined story images of a first father god as the cause of the environment, life, and the first humans.

Change

The Genesis Garden of Eden tale can be seen to represent a timeless place, and to be expelled from it is to enter relative time, the real curse of life and humans that causes all things to change. The first father god of Genesis made the human body good and in perfect order in a timeless place where there was no struggle or pain. The human body ostensibly inherited the ability to age and rot from the ingested fruit of the Tree of Knowledge of Good and Evil. However, all other life did not ingest the fruit but they also die. This is so as all living bodies are built on a foundation of parts that change over time, often and usually for the worst.

The human body is soft, solid, and composed of flowing distributing functions, composed of organs and cells, and atoms and electrons of energy that continually change and interact and exchange with the earth and solar environment, and with other living forms. All is a continuation of a cosmological force that moves and continually changes the seen and unseen universe.

All is held by time. The human brain subjectively arranges sensations to make a sequence of picture images as subjective time. Humans are also held in the grip of objective planetary and solar time of night and day, and further held in the grip of cosmological force as change of universal motion and time.

The ancient Greeks experienced and conceived a nonconscious moira or fate that conducts even the gods and each human to unavoidable experiences. Fate can be comprehended today to be the cause and effect conditions of life in an environment of time and change that conducts each to both a planned and an unplanned future.

Remedy

Having an origin from the earth, the subconscious functions of cellular life are a continuation of the environment. Life essence is a continuation of the earth and solar environments. The essence of life is a dynamic subconscious animating triune soul of forcible hunger for food, sex and reproduction, and aggression.

As a continuation of atoms and electrons of energy, and a cosmological force that moves the universe, the soul is resistant to destruction. The forceful soul can only be reduced by calming sensations of seeing, hearing, smelling, tasting, and touching, and the impermanence of conscious picture images, the brain ability for reasoning and comparison of images.

Humans are a psychological continuation with the environment. During life many are haunted by sensations of subject-object picture images of memory and future imaginations as a continuation from the environment, and though awake live mesmerized as if in a dream. A remedy for the unwanted or excessive picture images and the consequent symptoms of stress and anxiety, is all too often alcohol, and prescription or illegal drugs. A better natural remedy is the practice of meditation.

Meditation is the practice of holding attention steady in an effort to learn by observing brain content and function of sensations and picture images. Sensations are simultaneously subconscious and conscious, and more conscious when attention is directed to and focused on a stimulus. Willing behavior responds toward sensations of pleasure and away from sensations of pain.

Sensations of the senses continually change, as do picture images of experience, and forcible willing of hunger for food, sex and reproduction, and aggression. Since there is continual change from moment to moment, there is an emptiness to existence. Acceptance of this should lead to moderation for that which is wanted and loved, and bring each individual not despair but peace and poise.

Animating Factor

Writing in his book, *The Interpretation of Dreams*, Sigmund Freud (1865-1939) comments on his childhood difficulty of accepting the Jewish view of not having a soul.

"When I was six years old and was given my first lessons by my mother, I was expected to believe that we were all made of earth and must therefore return to earth. This did not suit me and I expressed doubts about the doctrine. My mother thereupon rubbed the palms of her hands together—just as she did making dumplings, except that there was no dough between them—and showed me the blackish scales of epidermis produced by the friction as proof that we were made of earth. My astonishment at this ocular demonstration knew no bounds and I later acquiesced in the belief...." (p. 238)

Freud's mother convinced him of the biblical Jewish view that the first two humans were made from only the soil of the earth, that there is no animating soul inside the body, and that the animator of life exists exclusively outside the body as a first father god. Later Freud became a medical doctor and this further reinforced his view of the nonexistence of an animating soul of life. Obtaining an education in medicine, Freud was to also become an atheist.

Following in the tradition of both Judaism and empirical science, there is no destruction resistant soul located in the human brain and body.

In the superstition of the monotheistic religions of Judaism, Christianity, and Islam, the only animating factor of life is a first father god who fashioned the life of the body that lacks a soul. The human cerebral cortex is represented by the intelligent first father god, and the dynamic of the soul is represented both by the Tree of Knowledge and curses from the god.

The imagined higher god of monotheistic religion is a projection of and represents the conscious content of the cerebral cortex of the brain. In monotheism there is only the life of the body sans a soul. Monotheism must by necessity be without a soul that animates the body on its own. A human animating soul encroaches on and reduces the authority of an external first father god as animator.

The monotheistic religions of Judaism, Christianity, and Islam foster dependency on an external animating first father god. Made out of only earth, humans are helpless and dependent on a first father. Therefore humans must be ethically good and pleasing for the first father's future judgement or the god will not resurrect, reanimate, or otherwise reward them. There is a total dependence on an external animator rather than on an internal animating function.

The force that assembles life is not a first father god. A monotheistic god is a creative artistic way of imagining the beginning of existence. The god as a beginning represents sexual reproduction and generations of forefathers and mothers. The only real way the origin of humans is human-like in any way, is in the sexual act of reproduction by evolving human ancestors. A first father god is a family and societal orientation to the beginning. As such the character of a first father represents the good of sexual pleasure that is not easy to refrain from.

The animating and assembling of life is immediately outside and inside the body.

It is not located far away nor is it a first father or human-like in any way. The beginning continues in the unfolding sequence of now, from the outside supportive environment. Further removed from but enveloping the environment is a supportive cosmological force. A continuation of a nonvisible cosmological force and the visible environment outside, occurs as a triune soul inside living forms. The inside of living forms is a continuation of the outside, as an animating and assembling triune soul. The assembler and animator of life is a supportive environment and an animating triune soul as a forcible hunger for food, sex and reproduction, and aggression.

Difficulty

For the average person, both physical body functions and cognitive processes are often difficult to comprehend. Individual experience is often a jumbled dynamic consisting of fleeting sensory sensations, picture images of the cerebral cortex of the brain, and willing for or against situations. The average person is often mesmerized into a waking dream state of remembering images of the past or imagining images of the future, and what to will and do next.

To sort out the confusion and uncertainty of life is difficult to do and personal access to an intelligent living person is hard to find. A first father god of all later fathers is easy to imagine and to accept, and for many is the facile answer to the difficulties of living. Far back in time, a first father god is imagined to exist as a powerful maker of the environment and life.

There is little long lasting comfort to be found on the earth. Therefore, many humans seek comfort from the origin of existence. Some comfort themselves by imagining a first father beginning. Then the idea of what is familiar can direct attention to humans, and humans can direct attention to the imagined first father god.

Reconnect

The English word religion (Latin re, again, and ligare or ligio, to connect) means to reconnect with where things come from. Monotheistic religions connect to an imagined first father, and since he made the environment and life, is a god. A monotheistic god is imagined so as to provide a simple identification for the origin of the environment and life. The god also provides care and protection, and dictates commandments of thou shalt and thou shalt not that guide individuals to maintain a semblance of ethical and moral social order. Praying to a first father is praying to what is higher.

What is real and higher is not a first father but the cerebral cortex of the brain that imagines a monotheistic god. The egoism of a god must be corrected by redirecting attention back to where the idea comes from, the cerebral cortex of the human brain. Not to correctly see that a first father god is conceived in the cerebral cortex of the brain, forms an egocentric lesion that impairs clear comprehension and reliable knowledge.

 The biblical first humans were made from the soil of the earth and thereafter all humans must return to it following death. Jews cannot escape the earth and the body must be resurrected on the earth by the god. Yet since a first father is imaginary and only subjectively real, an imagined god cannot and will not ever resurrect even a single supposed soulless body.

The imagining and acceptance of a first father god induces a patriarchal dependence. Following in the cognitively impaired patriarchal tradition of Judaism, Christians reconnect to the first father origin of existence through Jesus of Nazareth said by adherents to be the son of the god. Worship of the first father's son is a metaphorical way of connecting an individual with the imagined god.

The orthodox Christian message is that on earth there is suffering, and following the accumulated sorrows of life, there is an escape to an afterlife where there exists either reward or even more suffering meted out by a first father god.

In reality, the gospel or "good news" of Jesus is not so much the metaphor of an imaginary first father god and the resurrection of the physical body. The true gospel of Jesus is that an animating force exists within the human body that is resistant to destruction, survives physical death, and journeys to an afterlife dimension.

Buddha

The Buddha (623-543 BCE) taught a meditation discipline utilized to empirically observe and reduce the animating soul of life so as not to reincarnate again from an afterlife dimension to the struggle of existence upon the earth.

Buddha's struggle to awaken consisted of fasting from food to near death at one time during his search. After recovering, he established monastic rules of eating only one meal per day, not having sex, and not behaving with aggression. He is said to have reached awakening near the age of thirty-five.

Buddha could not and did not destroy the essence of life, the animating triune soul as a forcible hunger for food, sex and reproduction, and aggression. Buddha brought his life to a balance of function with the destruction resistant soul as it is a continuation of both earth atoms and electrons of energy elements, and a cosmological force that moves the universe and ever exists on its own.

Trees

Trees are often mentioned in the founding stories of religion. For example, in the biblical story of Genesis, the first humans obtained their basic knowledge from the first father god but they soon obtained more godlike knowledge from the Tree of Knowledge of Good and Evil. The biblical Garden of Eden tree represents the less conscious knowledge of the cerebellum, midbrain, and body that conflicts with the cerebral cortex and its imagining of the beginning of the environment and life to be a good first father god.

Disobedient humans were cursed by the first father who represents the cerebral cortex of the brain.

Jesus, the founder of Christianity and portrayed by the religion to be the begotten son of a first father god, cursed a fig tree. (Mark 11:12-14; Matthew 21:18-21) He was eventually crucified on a wood X or cross by Roman authority. A once live tree was cut down and assembled into the dead wood upon which Jesus was hung to his death. Christian doctrine teaches that Jesus suffered for the sins of humankind and yet his body was resurrected and rewarded by his first father god in an afterlife. Christian followers who suffer on the earth are inspired by this grim wood cross execution.

In vivid contrast to the gruesome role trees play in Middle East religion, a story about the Buddha's mother is that while on a journey, she gave birth to him in a grove of trees while supporting herself on a tree limb. The life of Siddhartha Gautama (623-543 BCE) who reached the status of Buddha, is also portrayed as connected with trees and the earth, the real and true origin of existence.

Buddha is portrayed as sitting under a tree after having achieved the bliss of nirvana. The Buddha sits on the ground beneath a live tree, connected to the origin of life, the earth. The iconography of Buddha portrays the message that the struggle of life on earth can be balanced so as to escape the disorientation of suffering and coming to earth again in a reincarnation.

In the three religious traditions of Judaism, Christianity, and Buddhism, trees serve differing roles. In Judaism, a tree the god had made contributed to bringing struggle and death on earth for humans and a bleak soulless body that returns to the soil to await resurrection. In the Christian mythos, the wood of a tree served as an instrument of suffering in life and contributed to death, and yet released the body to await resurrection. In early Buddhism, a living tree served to shelter the aspiring Buddha as he reached awakening while seated upon and touching the supportive ground, the only true and real origin of life; the energy elements of the earth.

Beneath the banyan tree he learned to discipline and reduce the animating soul of hunger for food, sex and reproduction, and aggression and by so doing to curtail a cyclical return to earth and life via the process of reincarnation. When dying his body rested between two Sal trees and was then cremated on a wood fire.

Animator

What animates life is not a first father god or human reason. What animates life is a nonreasoning forcible triune soul of hunger for food, sex and reproduction, and aggression. The triune soul is in continual adjustment and frequent agitation in life. Life is a continuation of the changing environment, and the greater cosmological motion of the universe, therefore precious little rest and comfort can be found.

Only the cerebral cortex of the brain and its ability for conscious measuring of reason and picture images can mediate, modulate, and attempt to regulate the body and the environment so as to enjoy relative comforts. The cerebral cortex of the brain seeks to measure, to reason and to order the environment into a better sequence of events and experiences.

To accomplish a better order, humans invent and make tools to improve life by obtaining food or being aggressive. For some dependent prone individuals and cultures, the cerebral cortex of the brain is utilized to seek order by imagining a first father god, who began a perfect sequence of order. The sequence of order made by the god was perfect but humans exceeded their basic endowed knowledge by obtaining more good and evil knowledge. To this day, humans contribute to and willfully cause much behavioral disorder to the environment and between and among other humans.

The first father god of Genesis is portrayed as bringing perfect order to the environment and humans, at least in the very beginning. The god then disordered the perfect order by banishing humans so that they continue to experience earthly disorder.

In modern times, the god is prayed to and asked to bring order to the environment, to bring social order, and to bring a healing order to the human body. To date, little or no real response has been forthcoming.

Joining

Joining with other humans in a group increases individual strength to accomplish chosen endeavors. Accepting an imagined first father god, increases individual strength to obtain chosen goals of personal and social order. Joining with an imaginary first father also brings reinforcement against the unpredictable events of the environment, and the irrational animating soul inside the body.

Humans invent real tools and also invent the tool of an imaginary ancestor god, a forefather who gets credit for bringing the first and best order of the environment and life. Humans get credit for bringing the disorder of a wicked world. In reality, there is no first father god maker of an only good order. In a non-monotheistic reality, there has only ever existed a relative good and evil order of the environment; for example a balance of rain and the disorder of drought or flood.

An imagined reasoning first father god obscures and conceals the non-reasoning animating triune soul that orders and organizes life. What is important to monotheistic religions is not immediate and real functions of the body but what occurred in a past time. For monotheism, based on Genesis 2:7, the body is said to be made only of earth and must be resurrected by a first father god. Monotheism orients to and emphasizes what is outside of the body, an artistically imagined first father, and ignores what is inside, a real animating soul of life.

The Aryan-Dravidian cultures of India exerted effort and attention to look inside at what animates the human brain and body. The practice of yoga postures and meditation were developed. Yet as far as the atma or soul, Hindu seers made an egregious error.

The Hindu social greeting is of upright hands pressed together and pointing to a person while uttering the word "namaste," meaning welcome, and said to also be a recognition and an acknowledgement by the person making the gesture of a divine presence within the person so greeted. The gesture is said to point to the "god within," meaning the atma or animating soul as a continuation of Brahman, a powerful cosmic force that expands and grows the universe.

The atma within a person is described as having three attributes, sat or true essence, chit or conscious knowledge, and ananda meaning bliss. This is an egregious mistake of attribution. While the human soul is a true essence, it has little ability for conscious knowledge and bliss. The Hindu greeting gesture actually refers to the conscious higher reasoning of the cerebral cortex of the brain, where a god or the gods are artistically imagined to exist.

Originating from and supported by the energy of the earth, the real animating force of the body is a forcible triune soul as a hunger for food, sex and reproduction, and aggression. Conscious knowledge and bliss occur in the conscious cerebral cortex of the brain when it manages to become relatively balanced and free of the subconscious midbrain and body, and the dynamic of an animating triune soul.

The best and highest realization, is that what animates life is not an imagined ego of a first father, exaggerated to be a god. An imagined first father is utilized to erroneously identify the beginning of existence and to provide a direction for conscious attention to seek care and protection.

What is real is that what animates life is a triune soul as a dynamic forcible hunger for food, sex and reproduction, and aggression. What is also real is that the triune soul of life is resistant to destruction as it is a continuation of the energy elements of the environment, and in turn is a continuation of a cosmological force that ever exists on its own.

Imagining a rational first father god is a way of seeking refuge from an irrational triune soul.

The soul is predominantly the less conscious cerebellum, midbrain, plexuses, organs, and autonomic nervous system of the body, and dynamically is a triune forcible hunger for food, sex and reproduction, and aggression. Not imagining and obsequiously seeking approval from an imaginary first father god, there can be clearly seen that what animates humans resides inside of them. Then can develop genuine compassion for each lonely existential self and soul.

Real

There are many parts of reality and humans have been long exploring, observing, and naming the many parts of the environment and living forms. Living forms are dependent on the environment and both are rooted in energy of atoms and electrons as a continuation of a greater cosmological force that ever moves a seen and unseen universe. Life is a continuation of primal force and energy blended with an animating acquired organic biochemistry of liquids and solids from the environment.

Based on observational reality, what is real is the environment and life. Humans have a dire need to see and comprehend how they are connected to each other and to the earth and solar environment. Yet reality is ignored for the monotheistic tradition of an imagined unreal first father god. Failing to accurately comprehend where the environment and life comes from, an unknown cosmological force and atoms and electrons of energy were instead humanized, imagined, and made into the human-like behavior of the first father god of monotheism.

There is no human-like god that animates humans and causes them to live and to do what they do. The real animating factor of humans is the supportive earth that is continued in life forms as an animating triune soul of hunger for food, sex and reproduction, and aggression. The soul is a continuation of the atom and electron energy of the earth, and is a continuation of a cosmological force that moves the universe. This being so, the animating soul is resistant to destruction.

Survival

To live and survive, the human body must obtain and eat food, must find a mate for sex and reproduction and mutual support, and must be defensively or offensively aggressive with words or behaviors toward other humans. The subconscious function of the body is an animating soul as a forcible hunger for food, sex and reproduction, and aggression. This animating dynamic is a continuation of the energy elements of the environment that is a continuation of a cosmological force. Being a continuation of energy and force, following death, by affinity and default the minimally conscious and mostly subconscious triune soul is saved to a dimension of energy and force.

Within a cosmological context an earthly dimension surely exists; therefore there is a probability that other dimensions also exist. Not supervised by a fear produced and imagined first father god, death is a natural progression of an animating soul from one dimension to another. A monotheistic first father god provokes strong human fears and concerns about acceptance, judgement, reward, and punishment.

The imagined monotheistic god effectively obscures the significant process of death. While the process of dying is uncomfortable and often painful, it is not a stop. Death is but a transition of the animating function of the body, a triune soul that is a continuation of the energy of the earth elements and the universal motion of a cosmological force that is unceasing and ever exists.

Training

To perform well, humans have to practice and train for both physical and intellectual tasks. The military and police perform mock training exercises, and actors rehearse their spoken words to train subconscious responses. To train response is the conscious intention to inform the subconscious cerebellum, midbrain, and autonomic nervous system of the body.

The subconscious learns slower than does the cerebral cortex of the brain and must be trained through repetition. Yet lesser conscious habit retains knowledge longer than cerebral cortex knowledge which is often forgetful. Even recent events are often forgotten by both young and old alike.

Conscious tasks are repeated to form subconscious knowledge. The conscious self of the cerebral cortex and central nervous system informs the subconscious soul of the cerebellum, midbrain, and autonomic nervous system of the body. Subconscious knowledge in turn directs much of conscious attention. The conscious self can correct and redirect the subconscious yet this is often difficult to do, for example to change eating habits. The conscious cerebral cortex of the brain wills the body toward or away from objects, while the subconscious cerebellum and midbrain wills the autonomic function of cells and organs of the body.

The subconscious brain and body functions are a continuation of, supported by, are conditioned by, and learn from a non-conscious environment. Conscious changing sensate impressions are retained and stored as picture images to become longer lasting knowledge of subconscious memory. To consciously train the subconscious to remember is to train the triune soul.

What Hindus and Buddhists call karma, is composed of the long lasting subconscious habits of a lifetime. The conscious intentions of living, train the subconscious triune soul to continue to pursue picture images of the cerebral brain. The soul will continue until each individual reduces subconscious habits and memories, especially of hunger for food, sex and reproduction, and aggression. Each individual has to save themselves from the habit of returning to life.

Training Attention

Sensations rapidly change, as do picture images of the brain. By training attention and adjusting it to stay relatively fixed or focused for longer moments of time, perception can better occur as intuitive knowing. Training attention, perception can function better as it is less impaired by picture images of memory and imagination of future.

Meditation is a way of facilitating perceptual not conceptual knowledge. Fixing of attention prevents memory and imagination from intruding upon perception. Attention can be trained to hover around an idea or problem so that a flash of intuition or perceptual clarity can occur in a novel insight.

Time

Calculating time by the phases of the moon is easier to keep track of than by observing the sun and where it progressively and slowly changes position as it appears on the horizon during a year. Like Asian and other Middle East cultures, Jewish culture utilizes a lunar calendar. Yet Jewish authorities do something quite different with the lunar calendar.

Edward Conklin

To keep the Jewish lunar calendar current with the solar calendar, a subjective and imaginary extra month is inserted into a real unalterable sequence of planetary night and day time. For Jewish religious authority to insert the imaginary month is easy to do, as for so long they have imagined a first father god who will reward or punish them, and might or might nor resurrect the physical body for the individual. The Jews subjectively imagine an extra month just as easily as they imagine a first father god as the origin of existence. An added imaginary month is treated as real and yet is merely a subjective mental tool.

To imagine, to make an image of a first father in story, is an artistic expression. To imagine a first father god is a work of art, an artistic expression of an image as an explanation for an unknown beginning of time.

Monotheists gather in a synagogue, church, or mosque to worship a first father god. What they unknowingly and really worship is the cerebral cortex of the brain that imagines such a simplistic human-like beginning related to humans.

Humans conflict with the environment, with other life forms, and with each other. If the cerebral cortex is not learned or educated, it is beset by ignorance and stupidity that exacerbates conflict. The subconscious cerebellum, midbrain, and body is dominant over and conflicts with the cerebral cortex. It is the non-thinking essence of a less conscious triune soul that causes much trouble for humankind. The conflict and disorder of human existence is a prime mechanism, a raison d'etre for the imagining of a first father god who can impose order on the sequence of relative change also known as time.

Life is fragile and is battered by the environment, other living forms, and by both a giving and unforgiving time. Time is what humans are tied to, the change of environment and the universal motion of a cosmological force. Every second dies, as does each minute, hour, day and night, and years, in an inexorable cyclic progression of life and death. Once tied to almighty time, no excuse suffices as each appears and disappears.

142

Some humans imagine and attempt to excuse themselves from the inexorable sequence of time by appealing to a first father god. By imagining a first father god, humans place themselves near to what is first and beyond time. What is human-like is first and best, more so than the secondary unhuman like environment and all other living forms.

Biological fathers really exist, as do grandfathers and also ancestor forefathers. In contrast, a first father exists only when imagined in the human brain as a primitive and poor effort to identify the beginning and time of existence. The human ego also seeks psychological protection in a first father beginning that in reality is a long evolving biological sequence of hunger and consumption of food, sex and reproduction, and aggression.

This is the dynamic forcible triune soul that is a continuation of the earth and solar environments, all traced to the universal motion of a timeless cosmological force, field, or ground.

It is the triune soul that should be rightfully respected and revered, not the mental conflation of human origin with an imagined first father god. Hail then, not to an imaginary first father but to the real animating triune soul of life. Hail to the many who have lived and died through inexorable time, not for a god but for food, sex and reproduction, and aggression.

Strife

The strife between a monotheistic first father god and human behaviors, is in reality the strife between the cerebral cortex of the brain, and the cerebellum, midbrain, and autonomic system of the body. A monotheistic god occurs only in the conscious self of the cerebral cortex of the brain.

As to the stronger of the two, the higher conscious self and the lower subconscious soul, the animating soul easily intrudes upon and interferes with the conscious self choices of the god-like cerebral cortex of the brain. Having an innate ancient pre-cerebral function of individual survival, the triune soul often contests with and wrests attention to turn to doing what is lower and not accepted as higher good deeds as sanctioned by a monotheistic first father god. The subconscious soul has primal priorities that serve self-interests and individual needs of survival.

Priest, ministers, rabbis, and imams are religious leaders whose primary function is to direct the attention of followers of a monotheistic religion, to a first father god who is imagined to be located outside of humans and beyond the environment. In reality, what religious functionaries are doing is directing attention to the higher functioning cerebral cortex of the brain where the first father god is imagined.

It is the task of monotheistic authority figures to persuade susceptible humans to imagine and accept that there is a numerical first father of all later biological fathers and mothers.

In promoting and urging the uncritical acceptance of a first father god, religious authorities direct attention away from the animating soul of the body and the earth. The triune soul is a continuation of the true supportive origin of life, the earth.

Behavior

Monotheistic religions imagine in artistic story that human behavior is related to the behavior of a first father god. In reality, human behavior is related to and is a continuation of the behavior of the earth, related to the behavior of the sun, to the behavior of the galaxy, millions of other galaxies, gravity, dark matter and energy, and black holes. All of these relative forms and functions are related to the behavior of a cosmological force that continually moves the universe and that ever exists on its own.

Life is ever connected to what animates it, to the nonvisible yet sensed energy and force of the universe. What is undying ever underlies the dying of all that exists. The reality behind the appearance of the environment and life forms, is a circular energy of elements, and behind these an evenly distributed cosmological force, field, or ground that ever exists on its own. As many dust particles visibly float upon an invisible air in sunlight steaming through a window, so do many stars, planets, moons, and material bodies float upon and through a cosmological force of the universe.

Drain the Swamp

The foul swamp of monotheistic religions must be drained. The inhabitant biting pests of mosquitoes, parasites, and snakes of various religious authorities that infect the blood of able bodied persons foolish enough to wander into the miasma of monotheistic thinking, must be eradicated.

The fertile soil of knowledge must be brought in to fill and build up a higher ground over the monotheistic low-lying swampland. No longer wandering through the mud swamp of ignorance, conscious attention can learn to clearly observe how the cerebral cortex of the brain imagines and projects a first father god to be the origin of the environment and life.

While the subjective imagining of a first father god uplifts human attitude, false hope must also eventually disappoint when no objective change occurs in response to prayerful pleading. Draining the swamp of monotheistic thinking, can contribute to better knowledge of the conscious self, and the less conscious and subconscious animating soul.

Problem of Knowledge

There is a problem with knowledge as illustrated by the biblical Tree of Knowledge of Good and Evil. Obviously knowledge can be used for good, and also evil as the excessive force of aggression. Knowledge is also both reliable and unreliable. Human knowledge must be acquired mainly through trial and error learning. Therefore, knowledge is faulty and mistakes are made that contribute to the problems and struggles of living.

There is also a problem with conscious knowledge in distinguishing between imagining and reasoning. Both function with picture images in the conscious cerebral cortex of the brain. The cognitive confusion between the two processes produces a first father god that is merely imagined, and is not at all a measured product of reason based on observation and experience.

Connect

Human life is a continuation of energy with the supportive environment and other life forms. This natural relationship is often unsatisfactory, frustrating, and painful. To counter this raw truth of existence, humans may seek other good humans to relate with.

Failing in this endeavor, some humans find comfort in imagining a first father who having a greater intelligence to make the environment and life, must be a god and also good. Humans forge a connection to the beginning by imagining it to be a good first father god.

The importance of having a first father god is a heartfelt but delusional effort to locate good in an environment of both good and evil experiences. To find a refuge of good, it must exist and be human-like in an unhuman-like environment. Based on surface appearances, it is notoriously difficult with limited human intelligence to distinguish what is good and what is bad or evil. By imagining an intelligent first father to exist, then the god can choose to provide answers to human questions and results to prayer requests for what is good.

Tribal Jewish storytellers could only artistically portray humans to be connected to and formed from the earth by a non-earthly first father god. (Genesis 2:7) During the twentieth century, the observational sciences of biology and physics have completely overturned the quaint tribal monotheistic myth and delusion of a first father god. The modern theory of evolution has traced the origin of life to the supportive environment of energy and elements.

Humans want to connect with what is good, and want to disconnect from what is bad and painful. It is often difficult to connect with what is good in the environment, and with good in other humans. Members of a monotheistic religion seek to escape a real environment by imagining a first father god who made it. To disconnect from the pains of life by resorting to imagining a good god is a bona fide delusion. It is not possible to reconnect with where things really come from by imagining a first father god.

Only in subjective imagining are humans connected to a first father god. To connect with what is real is to observe functions of the human brain and body, and the environment. Humans are connected to the real environment via an animating triune soul as a forcible hunger for food, sex and reproduction, and aggression.

Humans are connected to the earth and solar environment, to dimensions of energy and force, and to a greater cosmological force that ever exists on its own.

Disconnect

A salient significance and importance of excess suffering, sorrow, and loss is that the experiences serve to disconnect an individual from people, places, and things. Sufferings and sorrows can usefully serve to disconnect an individual from what is overly and obsessively wanted.

By focusing attention, the practice of meditation also facilitates a disconnection from the environment. To meditate is to disconnect an individual from what connects him to the environment. An individual is connected to the environment via sensations of the senses, and supplemented by the usual oversupply of picture images of now, past, and future of the brain, and connected by willing behavior.

What connects humans with the environment is sensation. The human brain organizes sensations of the senses of seeing, hearing, smelling, tasting, and touching into picture images that connect with the environment. Conscious willing for and against sensations and picture images connect individual behavior to the environment.

Conscious willing of the brain is supported by subconscious willing of cellular and organ body function that is a continuation of the non-conscious environment. Disconnecting from the environment through meditation, the conscious cerebral cortex better intuits how the body is connected to a real dynamic of force and energy.

Design

The philosophical argument of Intelligent Design or Creation Science, argues for the existence of a human-like god.

The simple argument is, since there exists an intricate design to the environment and living forms, there must also exist a designer, an intelligent first father god who designed and made the environment, life, and humans.

The major flaw in the Intelligent Design argument, is that it focuses on the order of the environment and fails to discuss the disorder. If a monotheistic first father designed order, the intelligent god must also have designed the disorder of environmental disasters, accidents, and diseases. The experience of disorder in the environment brings discrepancy and convincing doubt as to an intelligent first father designer.

What must then be logically considered is that in reality it is the intelligent cerebral cortex of the human brain that has designed a first father god in word and story format. The monotheistic first father is designed by and just for humans, as a simplistic way to comprehend the beginning of the environment, and to provide care and protection during life and death.

A monotheistic god is the subjective imaginary way an individual or culture identifies the beginning of existence and is how an adherent seeks to be saved from harm and suffering during the course of both life and death. The human ego imagines the greater ego of a first father god as an imagined way to feel special during the real non-special situations of life and death.

A monotheistic first father is an artistic subjective design, imagined by humans, to designate the beginning of the environment and life. A monotheistic god is artistically made with letters and words, designed by humans to provide an identity for an unidentifiable beginning of existence. A first father god designates the beginning of existence with religious verbal signage, a mentally made roadside sign on the human journey through the vulnerable and often unknown experiences of life and death.

A first father god is a human way of identifying and thinking about the beginning of existence.

The idea of a monotheistic god held by adherents, promotes doing what is good in an attempt to obtain approval and reward from an imaginary first father. In reality, the person seeks approval and reward from real family members, friends, coworkers, and society in general.

Monotheism

During times of helplessness, humans ask for and receive help from fellow earthly fathers. Sometimes human help is unobtainable or ineffective. Some humans may then, as have many in days gone by, turn to an imagined first father helper. Not receiving real assistance, turning to imaginary help is better than none at all. For early biblical Jews, as with many early peoples, daily experience was challenging and often a struggle. For Jews, it was not particularly uplifting to be told in the story of their origin that they were made from the soil of the earth. They were also told that they had no animating soul, only a shadow or shade that after death journeyed to the underworld of Sheol. There they would remain there until people forgot about them at which time the shadow entered the oblivion of the ever dark interior of the earth. The future was not especially attractive for Jews, until a physical resurrection was later added to their theology.

Better the palette of the past on which to paint an artistic work of a word story about a first father beginning. Sexual reproduction from the loins of forefathers and mothers was glamorized by imagining the long line of biological reproduction to have a first father beginning, who was further exaggerated to be a god.

The Genesis chapter one story of the beginning of existence, is artistically conceived in story as wonderful and good. Life was not yet a miserable struggle. It must have been reassuring to imagine that in the distant past, an intelligence must have made the environment and life. To accept that life has from the beginning always been a miserable struggle with no glorious beginning, would have been just too much to bear. How to brighten up existence?

Faced with the task of explaining the evil functions of the environment and life, the author of Genesis postulated a perfect order, and then in story told how human life became an experience of disorder.

Ancestor Worship

Monotheism, the accepted view of a first father god, is ancestor worship plain and simple. Evidence for this assertion is the prominent genealogy in Genesis (chapters 5 and 11) and those of Jesus in the gospels. (Matthew 1:1-17; Luke 3:23-38) The gospel of Luke traces Jesus back to the early patriarchal father Adam, and even boldly lists the very first father to be a god. Based on the biblical genealogies, tribal ancestor remembrance is plainly evident and is a psychological basis for a first father god. To worship a monotheistic god is in reality to revere the sexual reproduction of ancestors. The long biological line of human sexual reproduction was imaginatively made apparent by verbally clothing it with parental attributes of a first father god.

During a monotheistic religious service, a sermon is delivered to uplift listeners by mentioning the origin of existence traced back through a biological line of sexual reproduction, to arrive at a nonsexual beginning, a first father god. The long human biological heritage of making life with genitals, resulted in a body that ages and dies. This is deemed inferior, and must be glorified by imagining the making of the first humans from the soil of the earth by a nonsexual first father god.

Monotheism orients attention to an imagined good of patriarchal authority, a make-believe strong first father god maker. The ideational image of a caring first father is utilized as a dominating goodness that overrides the suffering and bad experiences of existence. A quick individual thought of a first father becomes a refuge of good during the immediate struggles of living. This is accomplished by directing attention away from the not good situation to what is all good, a strong first father glamorized to be a god.

Monotheism is a psychological fixation on an imagined father figure, a place to direct attention and be uplifted by imaginary care, control, and protection in the often uncertain and uncontrollable experiences of life. Attention directed to a first father is a mere mental resort to the cerebral cortex of the brain in an effort to alleviate discomfort and suffering by imagining the beginning of humans to be a human-like god.

Memo to monotheists: A god who will punish and harm humans is not good. Punishing curses were inflicted on the first two mythic humans during the fabled Garden of Eden beginning by the not so good god. So that the first father god does not appear too evil, a Satan and Devil is needed in monotheism to punish humans. The evil entity is a later added story character, a stooge who does evil work for and functions to deflect blame from the good god.

Why even speak of truth to humans when what is false is so much more comforting? A first father god even though imaginary is uplifting. Without a human-like god to accompany an individual, life is a much more risky and unhappy endeavor. The idea of a first father calms the stress of daily life by imagining that support and protection is available.

Imagine

The cerebral cortex of the brain organizes sensations into intuitive perceptions that measure objects in a space and time sequence of images. Reason is the ability to establish a cause and effect sequence, and to measure and fit parts of objects together, to invent. The conscious cerebral cortex of the brain can also conceive and imagine utilizing an analogical image. This is what monotheistic religions do when they rely on a lineage of real biological fathers as a basis on which to imagine a first father god as the origin of the environment, life, and humans.

In the past, Jewish storytellers used their artistic imagination to ameliorate their existence in the environment by imagining a first father god. Jewish religious authorities made use of the literary figure of a first father to dictate commands to control individual behaviors in their culture. The first father god is a literary mouthpiece that dictates commands in hopes of controlling the environment and as a hope to instill human social order.

Story Artists

The earth is a place of intense pleasures and pains related to eating food, having sex and reproduction, and aggression. To survive is the task of the less conscious triune soul of the midbrain and body, and to comprehend and live better is the task of the conscious cerebral cortex. While enabling survival, the animating triune soul contributes to the worst human behaviors in a ceaseless daily search for food, sex and reproduction, and aggression. The conscious cerebral cortex of the brain is shocked by the often cruel behaviors of the less conscious midbrain and body, and so it devises and imagines the false memory of a first father god story.

Lacking cognitive acumen, Jewish word artists became obsessed with imagining an origin story of a first father, and thereby overlooked a real function of an animating soul. By knowing a first father god outside, attention was directed away from a real animating soul inside the body. Jewish storytellers ignored the fact that humans have an animating soul by denigrating it to be the good and evil knowledge acquired from a fruit tree, and as curses from the first father god.

The good and evil knowledge portrayed as obtained from a tree by the first humans in the Garden of Eden story, is in reality the real knowing of the triune soul, an outgrowth or continuation from the earth as a forcible hunger for food, sex and reproduction, and aggression.

Jewish storytellers inverted the sequence of developmental events so that a first father god is portrayed in the Garden story as existing prior to the environment and life. The proper and real sequence of the origin of existence is that of the circular shape of atoms and electrons that are a continuation of the universal motion of a cosmological force. The circular energy of earth elements animate and shape the spiral form of genes and the circular shape of cells, to further evolve into multicellular life forms and humans. Evolving over time, humans began to tell stories of many gods and a first father god.

Biblical monotheism is a cognitively poor religion as it consists of the imagined story images of a god and a fruit tree that respectively represent the human cerebral cortex, and the animating triune soul that has its roots in and grows from the earth. The basic moderate knowledge first bestowed by the imagined god is the reasoning cerebral cortex that has the higher ability to name things in the environment. (Genesis 2:19-20) The knowledge of good and evil acquired from the tree represents a continuation of human growth from the earth, the lower triune soul of hunger for food, sex and reproduction, and aggression.

Overwhelmed by an outside environment and by an inside forcible triune soul, the conscious cerebral cortex of the monotheistic brain traces many forefathers back in time and then performs a leap to imagine (the mechanism of vaunted faith) the existence of a first father god.

The Genesis authors did one day imagine a creative way to identify the beginning of existence and to promote social order and reduce disorder. The artistic authors imagined the story of a first father god that over time developed into the monotheistic mythical religions of Judaism, Christianity, and Islam.

To find the best in fellow humans is often difficult to do. The best judgements and choices of the cerebral cortex are often affected and obscured by the forcible triune soul, the main task of which is survival.

Therefore, monotheists find it best to imagine a good first father god who made the environment and life to be good (Genesis 1:4, 10, 12, 18, 21, 25) and even "very good." (Genesis 1:31)

The cerebral cortex of the human brain is needy, needs reinforcement, strength, and greater knowledge of the environment and life and death. The cerebral cortex of early monotheistic individuals was limited by a lack of real knowledge and could only use a cognitive strategy to imagine and implore a strong first father for assistance in a good and evil environment. The cerebral cortex of the brain also assumes to control the animating soul of human life by devising a first father god who dictates commands to be obeyed by each individual.

Story Character

Attending a monotheistic religious service is a way that those attending say to each other, "I'll be good to you and you be good to me." This interaction occurs in the presence of an imaginary first father god who is all good and insists that humans be good to each other.

The Genesis story character of a first father god, artistically portrays the higher willing of the cerebral cortex of the human brain. The first human act of disobedience in the Garden of Eden represents the subconscious body that often and effectively resists obeying the cerebral cortex. The god could not have removed the acquired knowledge obtained from the forbidden fruit tree as it is the animating essence of life.

The over importance that the cerebral cortex assigns to its existence, is projected and assigned to an imagined first father god. The cerebral cortex must accept what is primal and what came prior to the godly cerebral cortex, the animating triune soul as a hunger for food, sex and reproduction, and aggression.

In the beginning, the triune soul supported by the earth evolved life and the cerebral cortex of the brain so that it could imagine a numerical first father god.

Testify

The distinction of the biblical Old and New Testaments began to be referred to by Christians circa 200's CE. The testaments purportedly and mainly testify that there is a first father god. In reality, the testaments bear witness and emphasize that the higher knowledge of humans is the cerebral cortex of the brain. Realistically, the testaments testify to the fact that a first father god is a psychologically imagined artistic product and is therefore only subjective real and not objectively real.

The biblical stories are false and misguided testaments to an artistically imagined first father god. A true testament would have to talk about the animating soul of life. The animating soul is artistically alluded to and portrayed in mythic story, and is not at all an intelligent and insightful expose of its dynamic existence.

Instead, the mythical first humans in the Garden of Eden are portrayed as disobedient. They picked the fruit of the Tree of Knowledge of Good and Evil, and thereby ingested, implanted, and infused within themselves the wicked knowing needs of hunger for food every few hours, sex and reproduction, and aggression. Humans put these wicked traits into themselves after obtaining them from the fruit of a tree fashioned by the first father god who placed it in the paradise of the Garden of Eden. Disobedience acted out by the first humans is a mythic storied way of expressing the fact that the cerebellum, midbrain, autonomic nervous system, and body, disobey the more intelligent cerebral cortex of the brain.

Story Knowledge

To know how the environment, life, and the first humans came to exist, would be important knowledge to have.

The only way to do this prior to modern empirical science was to imagine and artistically create a story of the beginning. Those who have knowledge of the beginning can then use it to inculcate and to control those who have little or no knowledge. Those who have the knowledge can also speak for the first father who began all existence.

For monotheistic religion, the only way to explain where the environment and life comes from, is to subjectively imagine a first father god. Observing the vulnerability of the human body, the biblical authors retreated into the past, and arbitrarily inserted a non-biological first father to be the imagined origin of many previous biological forefathers.

The Genesis authors projected their origin to be a first father god. An imagined good forefather is portrayed in story as caring for, protecting, and commanding his progeny to behave in better ways toward each other. This is an artistic way of overcoming pessimism and nihilism and of providing optimism on the often distressing journey through life and death.

Mess of Monotheism

The cognitive mess that is monotheism insists there is a first father god, and that there is no animating soul of the human body. These two witless errors of thinking are found in the claims of primitive monotheistic Judeo-Christian and Islamic religions. For the biblical Genesis authors, the animating mechanism of the soulless body is only outside of it as a patriarchal first father god. Only the god can animate life and reanimate a lifeless body. Ergo, there is no animating soul of the human form.

Having a heavy patriarchal dependence, and looking at a dead decaying body, biblical authors, imagined that only a first father god could resurrect (English prefix re, again and Greek anastasis, standing) or make the physical body stand again. For biblical authors, there is only a life of the body and there is no soul that animates and leaves the body at the time of death.

In the biblical Genesis story, humans are said to be made of dust and to dust they shall return. (Genesis 2:7; 3:19) There is no interior animating soul of the body, there is only an exterior animating first father god. The English translation of Genesis 2:7 states "…and man became a living soul." The passage suffers from a poor English translation as the biblical writers did not have the concept of an animating soul. Only the first father god could animate life.

The word translated as soul is the Hebrew word nephesh, meaning alive or a life. The English version of the bible translates the word as soul, yet the Hebrew word unequivocally does not have this meaning. One must draw the conclusion that the translator was inept, or that the false translation was even intended to deceive readers.

In the Jewish Encyclopedia under the heading soul, the article states that there is only a breath (ruah) that returns to the god who gave it, and the life (nephesh) that is in the blood (Genesis 9:4; Leviticus 17:11). The article also makes mention of the fact that the Jews had no idea of an animating soul until coming into cultural contact with the Persian culture circa 500s BCE, and Greek culture circa 300s BCE.

In the Catholic Encyclopedia under the heading of the English word soul, there is a list of the cognate words in other languages. These include Greek psyche, Latin anima, German seele, and French ame. There is a conspicuous absence of the historic biblical language cognates for the term soul, such as Aramaic, Hebrew, Jewish, and Arabic. This blatant fact reveals that the biblical languages have no word for an animating soul.

For monotheistic religions, the only animator of life is an artistically imagined first father god. The biblical authors prefer a superhero, a first father god and ignore the real origin of life within the body as the animating triune soul of hunger for food, sex and reproduction, and aggression. The soul is a continuation of energy from the supportive earth, and a cosmological continuation of force that animates the continual ever moving motion of the universe.

Nudity and Sex

In the biblical story of Genesis (3:10), the first two humans hid their nudity from the first father god. In reality, the god represents the cerebral cortex of the brain that disapproves of body nudity and insists on the necessity of covering the genitals since a social display of them easily entices jealousy, aggression, and the sexual act including forceful rape. Therefore, there exists the societal requirement and moral to conceal male and female genitals, and in modern times the breasts of women.

A first father god is merely an imagined way for the cerebral cortex of the brain to represent a long line of unknown previous fathers and mothers and their sexual activity. The biblical first father god is a way of valorizing a biological line of sexual reproduction and a consequent life of vulnerability, struggle, and suffering. Humans on some level of awareness realize that sexual reproduction provides more unhappy humans to experience struggle, pain, and the suffering of life.

The biblical storytellers also distanced themselves from sexual reproduction by imagining a nonsexual first father god, who yet has a penis as it is written that he made the first male human in his image. (Genesis 1:27) What does the god do if anything, with his male penis? Does the penis ever get erect? Of what possible use is it to him, and has he ever used it in any way? Perhaps he used it only once to become the father of Jesus? Might he in the future use his penis to again become a father?

The biblical god made the equipment of sex, human genitals, and so the male god has a penis. The god represents the origin of sexual reproduction via the collective genitals of the monotheistic group. The first father is an imagined story character by the cerebral cortex of the Jewish brain that represents the unknown origin of genitals and many multiple acts of sexual reproduction. . As a first father, the god represents a shared single act of sex and reproduction common to most living species that extends millions of years into the past.

The story of a first father and of the first humans obtaining sexual knowledge from a tree the god made, provides imaginary pseudo knowledge of what is a real sequence of evolved sexual reproduction. Monotheistic oriented humans like to think of themselves as coming from a higher first father god but in reality come from the lower act of sexual reproduction. Humans come from many forefathers and mothers supported by the unseen atoms and electron energy elements of the earth and sun environment.

Not What It Seems

Looking at traditional meanings of monotheistic ritual practices, alternative meanings can also be discerned. A rabbi, priest, minister, and imam, think of themselves, as do much of the public, to be like cheerleaders in support of a first father god. In reality, the monotheistic authority figures function to encourage and be supportive of others to utilize the higher ability of their cerebral cortex of the brain, both in its capacity for imagining and accepting a first father god, and in the making of higher reasoning ethical and moral choices.

Christians laud Jesus to be the son of a first father god. What is being said in reality is that Jesus is a son of the higher cerebral cortex of the brain, and not of a lower subconscious midbrain and body, the dynamic of which is an animating triune soul force of hunger for food, sex and reproduction, and aggression.

To get married in a monotheistic wedding ceremony is to promise to love and honor each other, performed in the presence of a higher first father god. What is really happening is making each other a promise to live in the higher level of reasoning in the cerebral cortex of the brain, and to live in higher ethical respect, love, and compassion. A phrase used during a Christian wedding is, "What God has joined together let no man put asunder." (Matthew 19:6) Mention of the god is a reference to the cerebral cortex of the brain.

In reality what actually joins a couple is the sexual attraction of the triune soul. Based on statistics, half of all marriages annually end in divorce and many remain unhappily married in ongoing conflict. Regardless of a lack of education, finances, health, or family situations, the main contributing cause of this emotional carnage is the subconscious midbrain and body functions of a dynamic triune soul of hunger for food, sex and reproduction, and aggression that animates and rules life.

Biblical prophets of the past strained through fasting and meditation, to focus attention on and to find a higher intelligent answer from a first father god. The individual sought answers to a myriad of personal and social problems of living. In reality, no first father god ever responds, only the prophet's own higher intelligent cerebral cortex provides an answer. The prophet therefore pretends to speak for a higher first father when in reality the words come from his own cerebral cortex of a physical brain. The biblical prophets sought guidance, received it from and spoke from, their own higher level reasoning located in the cerebral cortex of the brain.

The prophets spoke for a good social purpose but their prophecy was a ploy of perhaps unintended or intended pretense that claimed to interact with a first father god. Fasting and praying to get closer to a first father god, is to focus attention and restrict distractions so that the conscious cerebral cortex or subconscious dreams can reveal an intuitive and insightful answer.

The worship of a first father god is really the worship of the human cerebral cortex of the brain. The brain has the capacity to imagine picture images of now, past, and future, and has the ability to reason, meaning the ability to measure and shape objects. The adherents of monotheism then use the ability to imagine, to subjectively form the ideational image of a numerical first father god who has the ability to measure and shape the environment and life.

Meaning

There is an intended meaning of the mythological Garden of Eden story and there is an unintended psychological meaning. What is actually being said in the Genesis story is that life would at least be better and have more goodness if the cerebral cortex of the brain runs the show. The story character protagonist of the first father god represents the higher knowledge of the cerebral cortex of the brain that likes to think it is more intelligent and in charge of life. The cerebral cortex is the command maker and creator of words and artistic story of a first father god.

The antagonist of the god character is not the subtle serpent who is cursed to crawl on its belly, (Genesis 3:14-15) it is the artistically imagined growing Tree of Knowledge of Good and Evil rooted in the supportive earth. The tree represents the primary knowledge contained in the lower positioned trunk and limbs of the human body and its subconscious autonomic functions of breathing, heartbeat, digestion, and of life growing and evolving from the earth. The autonomic functions of the cellular body is the animating soul and is what animates and runs the show of life as a dynamic and triune forcible hunger for food, sex and reproduction, and aggression.

The live tree is a story character that portrays a living connection of the human body to the earth environment. The knowledge that the tree contains is that of the subconscious animating triune soul as an evolving continuation from nature. This knowledge is primary and trumps basic knowledge bestowed on humans by the imagined first father god character who portrays a real cerebral cortex of the brain.

The real contest of individual life has always been between the cerebral cortex of the brain, and the midbrain and body, between an imagined first father god and a real animating soul. What is good in humans is the godly conscious self and what is bad and evil is the subconscious animating soul as a forcible hunger for food, sex and reproduction, and aggression.

Putting aside patriarchal anthropomorphism for a sibling analogy, the talented conscious secondary younger brother is the imagining and reasoning cerebral cortex of the brain.

The younger brother must always answer to the primary elder brother but does not like to do so. Elder brother is the subconscious midbrain and body, the animating dynamic function of a destruction resistant soul.

Depth

How much light can be safely tolerated in such a dark and dreary human world? Pondering and looking deeply into the depth of existence may be disturbing and depressing for those who dare to do so. Looking at human behavior, and looking inside body and brain functions can be troubling.

The biblical word artists of Genesis must have been troubled. Finding some good on the earth and only a little good inside the human body and brain, the story writers then turned their attention beyond the earth to imagine a fatherly god who in the beginning made a completely good existence. The cerebral cortex of the brain was utilized to artistically imagine a first father god to cling to through the hazardous journey of life and death, as a way of being optimistic rather than pessimistic and nihilistic.

To say that existence was good at least in the beginning, raises an ongoing false hope of some imagined intervention and rescue by the first father. At least the thought of goodness serves as an imagined refuge from the bad and evil pains and sorrows of living. The thought of a good first father god also serves to comfort and alleviate individual fear and anxiety of impending death.

For biblical authors, looking inside the human body and brain at what animates it, to them life looked like a curse. Biblical authors failed to recognize the worse in humans to be an animating soul. Hunger for food, sex and reproduction, and aggression is the troubling essence of life. Therefore, the Semitic cerebral cortex of the brain turned to what is outside the body and distant in time, and proceeded to artistically imagine a first father god.

This is a way of praising and glorifying the cerebral cortex of the brain for its artistic ability to identify an unknown origin, and is a way of commanding an irrepressible and real triune soul.

Subjectively Real

A higher first father god is a subjective representation for the elevated cerebral cortex of the brain. The location of a first father god resides in the cerebral cortex as an artistic imagining and nowhere else. Faith and trust that a first father god exists as a subjective idea is true. To accept that a first father god exists objectively is false and a real psychological disorder.

A first father god is subjectively real as it is an artistic imagining occurring in the conscious cerebral cortex of the brain. What can be imagined as an image is subjectively real but not necessarily objectively real. The image of a first father god is an imagined beginning, and faith is the subjective acceptance of the first father artistic origin story of existence. When the subjective image of a first father god is accepted as actually existing outside the cerebral cortex of the brain, this is rightly termed a delusion, a mistaken idea that brings some comfort in the uncomfortable situations of life.

An imagined first father god is a subjective supportive idea of the conscious self, bolstered by group agreement and the comforting words of religious writings and leaders. Delivering the comforting message of a monotheistic first father god also pays rather well.

Daydream

Experiencing the uncertainty and misery of living, and with little hope for an improved future, only the past is open to speculation and imagination. Remembering a real deceased father or real grandfather, and perhaps even a great grandfather, and lacking further real evidence of what came prior, the Jewish brain then utilized artistic imagining and words to craft a story beginning of a first father god.

Not having objective confirmation, there remains only the wishful daydream and subjective feeling of safety on the shifting and changing seas of life. This occurs when a first father god is born in the cerebral cortex of the brain. A first father god is a pleasant daydream of the human cerebral cortex of the brain, a limited artistic way of knowing the beginning of a beginningless and endless nonhuman force that moves the universe. A first father god is a pleasant daydream of care and protection during the vulnerable existential situations of life and death.

Some but not an overabundance of caring, is observed to exist in human interactions of daily life. Seeking existential care and comfort during life and death experience, where should attention be directed? How about a look in the past? What could possibly care in the past, perhaps a memory of a parent or grandparent? How about imagining and daydreaming of a first father, a god? In this way, despair can be reduced if not avoided, and even a small bit of optimism can bring some existential ease.

The human daydream of praising a first father god, is praise of the real cerebral cortex of the human brain. The cerebral cortex of the human brain aggrandizes its own higher functions by imagining human origin to be a grand first father god. The origin of human life is deemed good yet human experience continues to be not so good.

In the mythical origin story of Genesis, the human body, primarily that of women, and secondarily that of men, is denigrated, shamed, blamed, and cursed. The imagined act is in reality the favoring of the godly cerebral cortex of the male brain that creatively daydreams the beginning of all existence to be a first father god.

The daydream of a first father god, serves to direct attention to the beginning of existence and thereby separates humans from their real and evil lower body functions of hunger for food, sex and reproduction, and aggression. The daydream of a first father god is a refuge of good sought as a response to the experiences of a not so good life and inevitable death.

The biblical word artists of Genesis sought to escape from the reality of a seemingly cursed body that due to their very limited cognitive ability did not contain an animating soul. The only way possible to reduce or escape the curse of bodily life based on the limited comprehension of the Genesis authors, was to imagine, daydream, and rely on an outside animator, a first father god. The daydream of a good first father accepted by many, continues to bring a modicum of solace and relief from life.

Original sin occurs only subjectively in the cerebral cortex of the human brain as a cognitive separation, a disowning and cursing of life. The cerebral cortex adjudges and projects the judgement that life is cursed by an artistically imagined story character of a first father god. The first father god of monotheistic religions is an image that represents the higher good of the cerebral cortex, and deluded adherents follow the pragmatic folly of locating a greater originating intelligence outside of the brain. The monotheistic way of finding relief from the existential situations of the environment and life, is for the cerebral cortex to daydream a first father god. The imagined god merely identifies and represents the terminus comprehension of the beginning of the environment and human biological reproduction.

The traits of the biblical first father god mirror that of humans and the triune soul of life. The imagined first father does not ingest food yet he savors the odor of overcooked meat offerings. (Genesis 8:20; 22:20-21) The first father did not sexually make the first humans but the god certainly has a penis as he did make the first man in his image. (Genesis 1:26-27) The first father also acts with aggression, such as when he cursed the first humans (Genesis 3:14-19) and destroyed most of life upon the earth. (Genesis 6:13, 17)

Taking Life

The earth and solar environment is both nurturing or good, and also uncaring or evil. As an evolved continuation of a good and evil environment, this duality is mimicked in human personality traits and behaviors.

The forces of the environment are observed to take many human lives during volcanic eruptions, earthquakes, storms, floods, and asteroid and comet impact. When gods are imagined to exist, they also are seen to like taking human lives. To get into accord or to appease nature or a god, humans seek help, want to gain favor, or avoid the forces of nature or a human-like god by sacrificing human life. Just as the environment and gods take human lives, so humans also take the lives of other humans through crime and war.

Dead Reckoning

For Judaism, and most Christian and Islamic religions, the dead rest and sleep until an unknown day of resurrection of the physical body. In contrast, for the Israelite Jesus there are "many mansions" (John 14:2) or afterlife dimensions. What animates the body goes to the dimensional mansions immediately following death as did Jesus and two crucified thieves. "And Jesus said unto him, Verily I say unto thee. Today shalt thou be with me in paradise." (Luke 23:43)

For some time there was for deceased Jews only an afterlife pit of Sheol beneath the earth. Following this conceived bleak end of life, eventually the notion developed of the rest and sleep of the remains during death while awaiting a resurrection of the physical body. For the Jews no animating energy exists within the body, only an external animating first father god.

Eventually, the Israelite Jesus brought the gospel, the good news to the Jews that what occurs at the time of death is a departure of an animating presence from within the body to transit to another dimension. Challenging the existent southern Judaic monotheistic political structure, the message of the northern Israelite Jesus was not welcomed. His message was too upsetting to Jewish tradition and so his life was terminated by the theological status quo. His afterlife teachings were soon diluted, absorbed, and covered over by the Jewish dogmatic tenet of a body resurrection scenario added to chapter sixteen of the gospel of Mark circa 330-360 CE.

Purveyors

Monotheistic authority figures set up their positions in life to be purveyors of good. The imagined good is a first father, a god who made everything. Monotheistic authority directs attention of adherents to what is good, a first father god who began the environment and life. In reality, sacerdotalists direct attention to the higher good of the cerebral cortex of the human brain that artistically imagines a story of a first father beginning.

The real worth of monotheistic leaders is that they teach simple-minded folk to identify and accept the origin of humans to be a first father god, and encourage the taking of refuge in the subjectively imagined and purveyed idea. What happens in reality is that faith and trust is promoted in the cerebral cortex of the brain to imagine a first father god.

Mistake of Monotheism

The English word mistake (Old Norse mistaka) has the following meaning:

"To miss taking what is intended, appropriate, correct, or right. A misstep, error or blunder of judgement or behavior caused by carelessness, deficient or insufficient knowledge, or poor reasoning. To misinterpret or misunderstand, or to misconceive. A deviation from accuracy or truth, to choose wrongly or incorrectly. To not take what is wanted or intended."

It is well known to each individual that sooner or later mistakes are made in life, some small and some large. During the course of an individual life, a variety of mistakes are made. Mistakes like shit, will always happen. Most mistakes are unintended. Some mistakes are beneficial and some are quite serious and harmful. There is a tendency to either underestimate or overestimate mistakes. It is good to recognize mistakes, when possible to correct them, to not repeat them, and good not to influence or to pass a mistake on to others.

Admittedly it is difficult to see or to recognize a mistake, to investigate, and to correct a mistake. It is difficult for most people to admit or confess a mistake, especially to themselves or to others.

Some mistakes are large and difficult to correct, such as the widespread mistake of monotheism. Monotheistic religion deserves to be classified as a mistake, a colossal one at that. Monotheistic religion is and will always be a mistake, a mistaken way of looking at the origin of the environment and life. Monotheistic authorities and adherents fail to recognize the mistake of a first father god, refuse to investigate it, fail to correct it, and intentionally promote, influence, and pass the mistake on to others.

The mistaken and incorrect view of monotheism so widely purported to be real and true, must be corrected. Monotheistic religion has been imagined by word artists and mistaken as real. As everyone knows, a work of art is an imitation of something. A first father god is an artistic conceived word story, an imitation for human comprehension of the beginning of time, environment, and biological reproduction.

It is a waste of time and effort to direct praise to an artistically imagined first father god. In reality, praise must be directed to a real animating soul as a continuation of earth energy and a cosmological force that moves the real ever moving universe. The real lord of life is not a first father god but an animating triune soul, a dynamic of hunger for food, fatherly and motherly sexual reproduction, and aggression.

The essence of human behavior is hunger for, obtaining, and digesting of food; searching for sex, reproduction and the caring for the results, and aggression as behaviors of construction, competition, and destruction. As a continuation of energy, humans have to continually seek food to replenish body energy to function. Humans also expend the energy of aggression with behaviors and words. Male and female are mutually attracted to the energy of sexual orgasm that forms life.

True Origin

The conscious cerebral cortex of the human brain must come to appreciate its true origin, not from an imagined first father but from a subconscious midbrain, cells, and organs of the body that exist as a continuation of an energizing supportive environment. Conscious willing is a continuation of and subservient to subconscious willing, the biological functions of the cells and organs of the body. The cells, organs and body function quite well without conscious intention, by healing wounds, digesting and expelling food and liquid from the body, and silently causing and conducting heartbeat and breathing, all without conscious intention.

The much more influential and more forceful function is the subconscious midbrain and body, the dynamic of which is an animating soul of hunger for food, sex and reproduction, and aggression. Emotion is the less conscious hormonal mover to action residing mediate between conscious reasoning and the subconscious nonreasoning soul whose function is cellular animation and survival. Conscience, a knowing with, is the subject-object conscious self, and is composed of at least some of the sixteen billion neurons of the cerebral cortex of the brain.

Lacking a discipline of learning, ignorance, a lack of knowledge by the conscious cerebral cortex is mainly and often evil. The person is then ruled by the subconscious animating soul, a forceful hunger for food, sex and reproduction, and aggression. It is the subconscious lower and lesser nonreasoning willing of the body for food, sex and reproduction, and aggression that disobeys the conscious higher reasoning and conscience of the cerebral cortex.

The human ability for higher reasoning may be woefully deficient or insufficient to acquire reliable knowledge. This deficiency is why in some less developed cultures, the cerebral cortex imagines a more intelligent first father god. The cerebral cortex of the human brain was in the past woefully insufficient in its ability to comprehend the workings of the environment, life, and the human brain and body.

In Middle East and European cultures, the cerebral cortex of the brain was limited and impaired by a lack of a method to observe, and so found it difficult to focus attention and to investigate the real environment and human brain and body functions. Instead, these early cultures utilized and relied on artistic ability to imaginatively create and to accept the word story of a first father god.

The monotheistic brain fails to observe the sensations of the senses, and to comprehend how they are transformed into picture images, and how conscious willing exerts effort for or against objects of attention. The monotheistic brain further fails to observe how human conscious willing is a continuation of subconscious willing functions of the body, and how these are a continuation of a supportive environment of energy. Instead, a meager intelligence imagines human willing to come from the willing of a first father god.

Turning attention to a first father god is to direct attention to the higher cerebral cortex of the brain and away from the lower midbrain and body behaviors. A first father god is an imaginative ideational effort to seek and expect answers, and to give thanks to for removing the limiting situations of living and dying. Solemn rituals and ceremonies to honor a first father god instead honor the genealogical line of fathers and mothers and sexual reproduction.

A sacerdotalist ostensibly speaks for an external first father god. In reality, the monotheistic official speaks only for the cerebral cortex of the human brain by urging others to act and speak on a higher level. This explains why religious functionaries are mere mundane and frequent hypocritical role models of acceptable behaviors.

The cultures that artistically imagine and accept a first father god, simply want individuals to act with higher levels of thinking and behaving. A first father god is an imagined role model that furnishes a direction for conscious thought to proceed toward in the less than half successful endeavor to find and to do what is good. The impaired human effort of ethics and morals is caused by the subconscious animating triune soul of hunger for food, sex and reproduction, and aggression.

Imagine

The cerebral cortex of the brain, the conscious self, attempts to save its own existence by the poor attempt of imagining a first father beginning. Faith and trust in a monotheistic first father god is in reality trust in the cerebral cortex of the brain to imagine the ideational story of a first father god who will save the individual.

Faith sustains the subjective imagined idea of a first father god but there is no objective reality. Faith must rely on a subjective idea or conception, not on perception of an observable object. The vaunted faith and trust that monotheistic religions insist on, is merely a cognitive effort by the cerebral cortex of the brain to accept the idea of a first father god and to maintain this unverified subjective view. Monotheism is the ideational effort to maintain an interest in and to feel better about living an unspectacular life, by imagining a spectacular first father god beginning.

The cerebral cortex of the human brain experiences difficulty in finding safety from the external environment and from what animates life internally, a triune soul as a forcible hunger for food, sex and reproduction, and aggression. The cerebral cortex of the human brain seeks a way to safeguard its existence by imagining a first father god.

Biblical word artists imagined a first father god that exists only in story. The imagined behavior of a first father god in story is an artistic overlay for the real behaviors of life and the environment. It is a real animating soul and supportive earth that brings life into existence. Life is ever prompted by a real animating triune soul that is a functional continuation of the environment. Inward hunger for food, sex, and aggression force humans to act with outward adaptive behaviors in the environment. Despite a monotheistic mythos, life is a continuation of atoms and electrons of energy that are a relative moving function and continuation of a cosmological force and universal motion.

Imagined by the cerebral cortex of the brain, a higher first father god represents the human yearning to be free from and to transcend the lower troubles of living, ageing, and dying. Life is a flawed condition as its animating essence is an internal triune soul, a forcible dynamic of hunger for food and water every few hours, sex and reproduction and its myriad distractions and dramas, and the aggression of behaviors and words.

Most people like to think there is something better to life than being forcefully directed by an internal hunger for food every few hours, engaging in sex and reproduction, and aggression and consequent struggles. What is better in real life is relief from life, from its existential angst of choices, conflicts, accidents, disease, disability, struggle, and ageing. This of necessity must eventually be death. As a person attempts to save life from death, so death is a way of saving an individual from life.

For monotheistic religion, what is better in life is a subjectively imagined first father god. The message of monotheism is that the higher cerebral cortex of the brain can triumph with care and love over the midbrain and cellular and organ body functions, the dynamic of which is the animating triune soul, and is that which ironically also saves the individual from oblivion.

A saving activity is attributed to and said to occur only by the performance of a first father, yet it is the animating soul that saves, not a god or a savior. In a reality of observation and not imagination, the soul is regulated by and is a continuation of energy and cosmological force. Observing a seemingly ever moving and ever continuing universe, the soul as a continuation of the cosmos also continues. The animating soul is a continuation of the momentum of atoms and electrons of energy and a cosmological force. Therefore the soul is resistant to destruction.

The conscious cerebral cortex of the brain makes picture images by transforming sensations.

As a continuation of a cosmological force and atoms and electrons of energy, it is this agglutinated mass of conscious picture images and a less conscious and subconscious soul dynamic that habituates behavior. Habit is a subconscious mechanism for repetitive continuation both in life and after death and therefore is a dynamic for dimensional survival and repetition. Since life is a continuation of universal motion, it is resistant to cessation and destruction.

The essence, the leftover, the remnant of life is the animating soul. At the time of physical death, the triune soul does not cease its animating function. As a continuation of atoms and electrons, and a continuation of universal motion of a cosmological force, only animation of the body ceases but not the animating soul.

Observing the eternal, the out turning, always and ever turning of the universe and probably multiverse, humans are capable of comprehending their connection with this seemingly infinite motion. Infinite motion continues as real relative motion of atoms and electrons of energy that mass to form the rounded rotation of the earth. The energy of living forms is continually replenished by an intake of food and water from the environment.

Waiting

The cerebral cortex of the human brain has evolved to the stage where it will soon give up waiting and relying on the artistically imagined word stories of a first father god of monotheism. Instead humans increasingly rely on their own demigod intelligence consisting utilized in the scientific method of observation and testing to invent and innovate in many fields of endeavor. The cerebral cortex has evolved and increased its ability to obtain real and reliable knowledge and to depend less and less on a word artist imagined first father god.

One first father god as the origin of existence, is imagined by the cerebral cortex that artistically represents its unknown origin by making it known through use of words and story.

Let those members of the monotheistic folk religions comfort themselves with the subjective idea of a first father while waiting for the god to show up and to lend a hand. Waiting will surely be in vain such as occurs in the play, *Waiting for Godot*, written by Samuel Beckett (1906-1989).

Know Self

History records that two sayings were inscribed over the Greek temple of the god Apollo at Delphi. These are "Not Too Much" and "Know Self."

The first admonition is variously translated into English as to be temperate, nothing in excess, or all things in moderation. The saying (Greek meden, no or not, and agan, much) literally means, no much, or not too much of anything. For the average person this is most difficult to do. Of course this can include many areas of experience such as eating food, having sex, expressing aggression, and worry. Not too much of things or temperance is mainly a focus of attention on the moderation of behaviors and external objects.

The second admonition (Greek gnothi, know, and se, to or for, and auto, self) is undoubtedly the most difficult as it means to know the individual human self. While difficult to learn about external things, it is even more difficult to learn about what is innate. The Greeks had few methods to enable them to explore and know the internal functions of the brain and body. There was no introspective or meditative method to investigate the internal self. Today there are developed enhanced ways of knowing the internal self of the human brain and body through surgery, blood tests, psychological testing, MRIs, CT Scans, and X-ray, just to name a few.

For the early Greeks, to know the self was not easy to accomplish. It continues to be difficult for an individual to know the dynamic self during the busy course of modern life. For animal species, including humans, attention and learning consists mainly of a focus on external objects.

Animals lack the ability to focus attention on and to observe internal brain and body processes. The mass majority of humans lack the ability to introspect, to observe internal mental and physical processes. What occurs inside the individual is ignored and little learning of the self takes place. External objects are deemed more real while internal parts and functions are less real as they are not observed beneath the skin surface covering.

What an individual is are the store of conscious and subconscious picture images in the cerebral cortex of the brain. The individual is primarily the animating triune soul of the midbrain and body as the dynamic triune soul of hunger for food, sex and reproduction, and aggression.

Attention is usually not trained and directed to steadily observe internal brain and body functions. Attention is not directed to the dynamic of sensations of the senses, and how these are transformed into picture images. Attention is not directed to the conscious willing force occurring in the brain as conscious intention. Attention is not directed to observe the body and so there is a consequent ignoring of the animating dynamic of life as a triune soul of hunger for food, sex and reproduction, and aggression. What animates both conscious brain and body processes is a subconscious dynamic triune soul as a hunger for food, sex and reproduction, and aggression.

Attention is not directed to how life is supported by and is a continuation of the energy elements of atoms and electrons of the environment. Attention is not direct to observing how moving parts of cellular and organ life function is a continuation of atom and electron movement. There is also a failure to direct attention to how all relative movement is a continuing motion of the universe.

Through life individuals exert conscious willing for a situation to be or not to be. The triune soul is a dynamic constellation of hunger for food, sex and reproduction, and aggression that wills for and against. As a continuation of atoms and electrons of the environment and a cosmological force, it is therefore resistant to destruction.

The soul is a continuation of energy and force, and individual willing is laid down as a habit to survive. The animating essence of life as partly conscious and mostly subconscious, is resistant to destruction.

Comprehending this to be true, during meditation, there must be a consistent training and gradual reduction of straining for or against. The insightful meditator does not overly strain for or against the sensations of seeing, hearing, smelling, tasting, and touching. He does not overly strain for or against picture images of now, past, or future. He does not overly strain willing for, and does not overly strain willing against. The causal result is equilibrium, nirvana.

Self and Soul

Not an imagined first father god but the real conscious human self must do its best to make its way through the disappointments and pitfalls of life. The conscious self must also work to direct and discipline the less conscious and subconscious animating soul. Few humans ever become cognizant enough to glimpse the existential task and even fewer make the effort and work to increase personal comprehension of the self and soul dynamic.

It is evident in life that the less conscious and subconscious animating soul as the dynamic of hunger for food, sex, and aggression, usually prevails over the conscious self. The less conscious or subconscious midbrain and body is more important than the conscious cerebral cortex as it runs cellular function and movement and works for survival, while conscious attention functions mainly to observe and both to imagine and reason.

When the conscious self prevails over the soul, the result is a good, ethical, and moral person. When the self further prevails over the soul, the result is an exceptional person traditionally referred to as a saint. When the conscious self prevails among members of a group or society, then creativity and peace may reign, but not anytime soon.

Disorderly Life

In the first few chapters of Genesis, the non-biological and not from the earth first father god of monotheism is given credit for order, and the first earthly biological humans get credit for the disorder of life. The primitive artistic imagined story of Genesis has through modern times grown into an accepted monotheistic tale of history.

An imagined rational first father god is the human artistic effort to be more rational. Marginally rational humans utilized artistic ability to imagine a rational first father god. The barely rational biblical word artist uses artistic word imagery to insert a rational first father into a sequence of an irrational biological function of hunger for food, sex and reproduction, and aggression.

This is the animating triune soul that forces life to live as a continuation of the atom and electrons of energy of the earth, and in turn is a continuation of a cosmological force that moves the always moving universe and ever exists on its own.

The pragmatic way for biblical authors and monotheistic adherents to acquire a more orderly life is to artistically imagine and appeal to a first father god who imposes order. The imagined good of a first father god artistically composed by word imagery in the first chapter of Genesis, has to be immediately followed by the calamitous words of chapters two, three, and four that describe a consequent disruption of the original good order by the disorderly conduct of the first humans. A first father maker of an imagined uber order is praised while humans are blamed for the disorder of life.

In the real order and disorder of the environment and life, is inserted the artistically imagined ordering by a first father god. Searching for order, the biblical authors and word artists could only imagine it to have occurred in the generational past of just several thousand years.

A barely rational Iron Age Semitic cerebral cortex of the brain artistically imagined a rational first father god.

Praying to a first father god is in reality imploring and asking for the cerebral cortex of the human brain to bestow the good of comprehension and order, and to reduce disorder. The reaching out to an imagined first father god is the reaching out of the cerebral cortex of the brain to receive a higher reasonable, measurable, and workable answer to existential problems. The focus of attention on the ordering and arranging ability of a first father god, is the attempt to vicariously evoke personal order in the disorderly experiences of human living. A role model of rational order reinforces the marginal rational order of the human cerebral cortex of the brain.

Recalling a past order by imagining a first father god is an artistic way of imposing order during the disorders of life. Yet this maneuver, however inspiring, is only subjectively successful. An imagined first father god of order is a way of locating and holding onto some previous good order in a disorderly environment, and the disorders of life such as accidents, illness, ageing, and death. The false hope of monotheism is that the great first father imposer of the order of existence will restore order to the disorder of life and death. The only monotheistic cure for the disorders of ageing and death is an imagined resurrection of the body.

A first father god is an artistic way of imagining where order comes from, how human disorder began in time, and how humans can obtain order in their daily lives. The good order of a first father is only an imaginary way of locating and obtaining physical and psychological order. To imagine an external first father god who orders the environment and life, is an attempt to bring internal order by emphasizing the cerebral cortex of the brain to influence body behaviors.

What makes order? The monotheistic answer is, a first father god. What makes disorder? Certainly not the good god. Humans first made disorder caused by their disobedience, and have been doing so ever since. Later a Satan, Devil, or Lucifer is portrayed as making the disorder of existence.

The generation of life is easily imagined to be a rational first father god. In reality, a generation is a "gene rational" order of human biological reproduction animated by a triune soul as a forcible hunger for food, sex, and aggression.

For the real universe the single imposer of order and disorder of the environment is a cosmological force, and the energy of atoms and electrons that compose material forms. The real imposer of the order and disorder of life is the animating triune soul as a forcible hunger for food, sex and reproduction, and aggression. Both the semi-orderly function of life and the disorderly conduct of life is imposed by the animating soul. Each person eats, fucks, and fights their way through the pains of life as best they can.

Legal and illegal drugs are an individual effort to experience a temporary pleasure. Addictions are for those who cannot order their life for real, and instead do so artificially with drugs, alcohol, food, possessions, and relationships.

For humans, the environment both orders and disorders daily life, as does the animating triune soul both orders and disorders individual life as a forcible hunger for food, sex and reproduction, and aggression. A real animating soul causes much of the disorder for humans. Therefore, the cerebral cortex of the brain imagines a fatherly god who first made order, and later dictated orders of the commandments to be followed.

The human cerebral cortex that artistically portrays the beginning of existence to be a first father god, approves of order and disapproves of the disorder of the human midbrain and body. The god's disapproval is expressed by cursing the first two biblical humans for their disobedience. A first father god is the answer provided by monotheistic authorities to fearful and needy humans who want to maintain order and to survive the disorders of life and death.

A biblical fatherly god first imposed order after death by making the pit of Sheol, (Genesis 37:35) a place for the shadow or shade of the person to dwell following physical death.

When people forgot about the deceased, their shadow blended with the ever darkness and oblivion of the earth's interior. Circa 600 BCE the prophet Hosea (6:2) first announced that the fatherly god will resurrect the dead, as did the prophet Daniel (12:13) circa 200-100 BCE.

Influenced by Jewish dogma, an Israelite son by the name of Isho or Yeshua, Greek Jesus, (circa 10 BCE-33 CE, see John 8:58) is portrayed in the gospels as having had a bodily resurrection. Yet he disavowed a body resurrection by announcing that there are many dimensions of an afterlife paradise and that entry to them occurs following physical death. (John 14:2; Luke 23:43)

Under Judahite influence, scribes portrayed Jesus as resurrecting in the physical body rather than portraying the soul as leaving the body. The Israelite teacher Jesus realized he had an animating soul and this obviated the need for a body resurrection. Word artists portrayed the drama of the physical body coming to life again as it was easier to do so. To portray the soul as actually leaving the physical body would have been most difficult.

Jesus is said to be the son of the maker of an originating good order. As such he is portrayed as bringing the order of healing and life to the disorders of disease and death. The two commandments uttered by Jesus were intended to instill order by loving an imagined shared first father god of origin, and to love neighbors as oneself. Both are intended to lessen the disorder of social living.

A monotheistic first father god is a crude way primitive humans acknowledge they share the same origin and are a member of the same group. A monotheistic first father god is a rallying point for at least half of the human family population, as an uncouth way of acknowledging a shared origin and relationship with each other. The scriptures of monotheistic religions are a prescientific artistic use of words as a way of imagining and comprehending the order and disorder of the environment and life.

Criminal and civil laws are better pragmatic ways to bring about social order. Modern science is an observational way of testing and comprehending order, and to find ways to improve the order and reduce the many disorders of living. Humans do share a common origin with all of life.

Not via a first father god but as a continuation of a shared supportive earth of atoms and electrons of energy, and further shares a continuation of universal motion from a cosmological force that ever exists on its own. To focus attention on an imagined first father god, is a poor attempt to obtain personal physiological and psychological order. Only a method of observation and reasoned response can bring about personal order, and naturally this has limitations.

Meditation practice is one such methodical discipline of observation. To focus attention on an internal sensation such as breathing, reduces picture images of past and future. Focusing on the sensation of breathing reduces imagining and reasoning, and if the meditator does not fall asleep, can descend into a relaxed less conscious level where dreams are formed, and may also receive seemingly amazing clairvoyant and telepathic impressions. To observe and study the strong force of hunger for food, sex and reproduction, and aggression within the body, is to gain knowledge of the animating soul.

While the common people of India implore gods and goddesses for assistance in living an orderly life, Hindu seers developed the method of yoga and meditation to observe, discipline, and correct some of the disorders of brain and body functions. A son of India known as Buddha (circa 623-543) awakened to the correct fact of the disorder of life that he referred to as dukkha. He taught a way to achieve order of the brain and body by the discipline of meditation, eating one meal daily, celibacy, and love to reduce aggression.

Buddha practiced ascetic disciplines as he wanted to stop or remove his hunger for food, sex and reproduction, and aggression.

Yet he eventually came to see as he neared death from fasting that the animating triune soul is the essence of life and is resistant to destruction. He wisely chose a middle path of not going to extremes. His conscious self balanced his subconscious animating triune soul.

Humans have to habitually deal with the triune soul of a forcible hunger for food, sex and reproduction, and aggression. To further complicate the existential situation, each individual has to deal with these traits in others in varying situations. What a mess! The dynamic of hunger for food, sex and reproduction, and aggression keeps each individual from a condition of poise and balance. There are only brief respites from the jostling change of living.

Order in now moments comes by regulating brain and body functions. Eating and exercising reduces disorders of hunger and health, knowledge reduces the disorder of ignorance, acquiring money reduces the disorder of poverty and debt, and relationships reduce the disorders of loneliness and lack of support. To reach a level of individual order in both the environment and within the brain and body, is the summum bonum of life.

Battle

Life is a short or long battle consisting of a series of battles to exist. That this is so is comprehended by few. There are physical and mental battles. There is a battle to keep healthy, a battle to acquire knowledge and reduce ignorance. There is a battle to compete in work and acquire money, and a battle to have and to maintain relationships of family and friends. The conscious self battles with the animating subconscious soul in its efforts to acquire food, to have sex and reproduction, and the daily small and large acts of aggression.

In the battle that is life, some imagine a first father god as a destroyer, warrior, a protector, and raiser of dead bodies. For Christians the first father is a lover of humans and literally had sex with a human woman to intentionally have a son. The first father god exists to assist humans in the battle to survive life and death.

The human cerebral cortex of the brain imagines its origin to be a first father god. A first father portrayed in monotheistic scriptural story is an artwork. Biblical storytelling word artists portray the beginning of existence to be a first father god for the dual purpose of identifying an unknown origin and protection.

The prevalent false drivel of monotheistic writing and thinking must be cleaned up; an arduous and difficult task somewhat reminiscent of Hercules cleaning the Aegean stables. The pompous representatives and stand-ins for an imagined first father god must fess up to what they really are, advocates for an artistic story theory of the beginning of existence.

Pleasures

Individuals go from pleasure to pleasure all the while amid chance, risk, danger, and disaster. The pursuing of small pleasures keeps each individual progressing in the forward movement of living. Human attention is mainly on the pleasures of consuming food, sex and reproduction, and the competitive verbal and physical aggression to succeed.

Eventually, to each and all, tiredness of petty pleasures ensues. Repetitive pleasures soon lapse into unsatisfying boredom, and unless alleviated increasing to painful frustration, and may further progress to aggression and destruction for oneself or others. Wandering through the dark ways of life dismays and slows the pace of living, distracts and may even push an individual off course, to sideline with concern and despair, so that the only effective way of rescue is the eventual relief of death.

Relative

John Benjamin Conklin (1825-1870) a Spiritualist medium, in 1858 conducted a séance at 477 Broadway in New York City.

Attending were several people including Emma Hardinge who received the communication from a deceased spirit that "Immortality in the light of Gospel teaching is a fiction." (Banner of Light. Vol. III. 3/18, July 31, 1858. p. 7) In support of a distant relative, the received communication is correct, a body resurrection by a first father god and consequent immortality of the body is a fiction. The fiction of resurrection was added to the gospel stories of Jesus, who it seems went directly to heaven when he died on the cross. In fact he promised the two thieves that they would join him that very same day. "And Jesus said unto him, Verily I say unto thee. Today shalt thou be with me in paradise." (Luke 23:43)

Spiritualism accepts no first father god or a savior son to save an individual. However, Spiritualism drags in an Infinite Intelligence that mimics the personality of a first father god. Spiritualism is a break from the fiction of body resurrection. The deceased go to an afterlife dimension from where they can also communicate with the living through a medium. Spiritualists do advocate a "spirit" resurrection. Spirit means breath, which is a mere metaphor for an activity in the body that survives. Yet like most every religion that exists, Spiritualism throughout its brief existence fails to define what a soul is and where it comes from.

The religion of Spiritualism has no creation story. There is no explicit mention of where the soul comes from. It is assumed that the soul is somehow related to the hyperbole presence of an imagined human-like Infinite Intelligence. The reality is that the animating soul is a continuation of what is observable and real, the environment, and universal motion. Life is animated by and is a continuation of the atoms and electrons of energy elements of the environment and not otherwise by a first father god. That the body is a continuation of the elements is evident in the fact that it requires food and water every few hours to replenish its energy. All of the universe is in motion, animated by a cosmological force that extends through all dimensions and ever exists on its own.

Soul Dynamic

The animating soul is a dynamic force of survival. Human conscious reason cannot measure the soul or picture it, and can only discern and observe its function. The triune soul is a timeless and imageless force yet images are reflected in it. Conscious reasoning fades, and picture images of comprehension lessen, as attention approaches the soul so as to better comprehend its function and origin. Conscious reason soon steps aside when the subconscious master of life, the animating soul forcibly makes its presence known. When the triune soul seeks what it wants, food, sex, and aggression, reasoning images are pushed aside. Conscious reasoning occurs mostly by use of images that measure space-time objects.

The soul can force opposing images out of the way making it difficult to remember and to plan reasonable actions and to think clearly. To survive, the subconscious soul easily impairs conscious reasoning, hijacks it, and moves it to the sideline. When the subconscious soul turns attention to what it wants, it forces the conscious self to make picture images of what it seeks to acquire.

The subconscious soul easily pushes the conscious self around. Yet, the conscious self can also modify, push back, and redirect the soul to accept a substitute satisfaction. The dynamic soul mainly wants good food but the conscious self can modify response, and if need be to survive, may guide it to scavenge and even to cannibalize. The soul wants sex with a suitable partner and may want to biologically reproduce children but if not available the self may settle for masturbation and adoption. The soul may want to express aggression toward someone or something but the self may settle for a substitute person or object, or instead of physical behavior may direct aggression verbally.

Humans are forced to act by the animating soul of life, preferably for good but just as easily for the excessive force of evil. The real problem of life is not as fear based monotheistic religions insist, to have a first father god resurrect and save the body, or as popular religion insists, to save the soul.

The real problem of life is to consistently use conscious reason to balance and to firmly reduce the forcible subconscious soul, and to provide pragmatic and good directions for it to proceed on the journey of life and death.

Journey

Most live a life of daily distractions. Few ever begin a personal journey to comprehend life and death. The journey must begin by practicing a discipline of meditation that observes sensory sensations that transform into conscious brain contents, picture images of now, memory, and future. Further along the journey can be observed that by meditatively reducing conscious picture images, attention can find a place where dream images are formed and appear during sleep. This place is the untapped potential of humankind, a place of creativity, and extra-sensory perception of telepathy, clairvoyance, and prophecy.

A meditative individual might be fortunate during the journey to arrive at a distant overlook, and here may observe a less conscious and subconscious essence, a triune forcible hunger for food, sex and reproduction, and aggression. When calm and restive, the ancient essence of the soul may be observed to be a dynamic imageless containment of residue images. The conscious self must learn to observe the less conscious and subconscious soul to be what survives death. The soul is a continuation of the atoms and electrons of energy of the earth and solar environment, and is a continuation of a destruction resistant cosmological force that moves the universe and ever exists on its own.

Value and Worth

Obviously the human body is not valuable as following physical death it is placed in the ground to decay, or it is cremated by fire and reduced to ashes. Surely then, though it is mourned after death the body is not worth much. Can the picture image contents of the brain be worth much more than the physical form?

Internal sensations change second to second, and as do picture images, and as do for better or worse, physical willing behavior of the common person who manages to achieve little of importance through a lifetime.

Daily devaluation of human life occurs as accidents, crimes and wars, addictions of many kinds, and physical diseases and mental disorders. A first father god is a way of making the low value and low worth of life to be higher and more worthwhile. A first father god valued by humans is a human way of valuing human life. Imagining a higher first father god is a human way of giving worth to various lower human experiences of living.

However, odes and hymns to the origin of existence should not be sung in praise of a first father god but to the cerebral cortex of the human brain that uses words and story to artistically imagine a beginning of the environment, life, and humans. Many more odes and hymns must be sung in praise of an animating triune soul of hunger for food, sex and reproduction, and aggression.

Life is a continuation of supportive energy, the atoms and electrons of the earth. Life is also a continuation of a rarified cosmological force, knowledge of which is difficult to come by but that must of necessity be inferred to exist and to ever continually move a universe of unceasing motion.

Legal Complaint

A first father god is a way of comprehending the unreasoning origin of the environment and life, and is a way of making existence reasonable. A first father beginning is a way of bringing comfort to an uncomfortable life, and of making it tolerable.

However, an unobserved beginning imagined and artistically portrayed as a first father god, and purposively presented to be true and factual, distorts and harms psychological comprehension of the human existential situation. Monotheistic religion therefore, to use a legal term, is a fraud, defined as:

"A false representation of a matter of fact, either by words or conduct, by use of false or misleading allegation, by concealment of what should have been disclosed that deceives or is intended to deceive an individual so that the person will act on it to his or her personal or legal injury."

Based on this definition, monotheistic religions should be charged and indicted for defrauding of the general public. The complaint should also include the charge of collusion, defined as:

"An agreement between two or more persons, who usually covertly conspire to commit an illegal act of fraud. Any results brought about by the collusion are considered to be legally void."

Monotheistic authorities have in the past and continue daily to cooperate and to encourage humans to accept the tradition of a first father god. Monotheistic leaders also gather to promote faith that the idea is true and that a first father god exists and is real. The origin of existence portrayed as first father god is a ruse and intentional misrepresentation.

The charges against monotheism is the fraudulent misrepresenting of the origin of existence to be a first father god. Monotheistic religion is a fraud, perpetuated by the collusion of authority figures and their intentional and continuing misrepresentation of the beginning of existence to be a first father god. As such, monotheistic authority figures must be charged and prosecuted for fraud.

Monotheistic religious leaders must also be charged with grand larceny and a felony. Over many centuries, much money has been received in collection plates and left in personal wills to benefit monotheistic authorities who have falsely advocated a first father god to be real. The active promotion of monotheism is also, in a sense, a theft of valuable human psychological comprehension.

The evidence for monotheism is nil, only tradition exists from early primitive times and a vaunted faith.

Faith (Latin fides, trust) is defined in two differing translations of the New Testament verse of Hebrews 11:1.

"Now faith is the substance of things hoped for, the evidence of things not seen." KJV

"Now faith is confidence in what we hope for and assurance about what we do not see." NIV

The King James Version states that faith is the subjective substance, the only firm part of what is hoped for. It is also said that faith is evidence of what is not evident or is unseen. In other words, if you have the idea of a first father god, then it must exist. Well this is surely flimsy evidence for the existence of a first father god. Many subjective ideas exist for which there is no objective and real truth, such as Santa Claus, the Easter Bunny, mermaids, and the tooth fairy. Merely having the subjective idea of something furnishes no firm ground for acceptance of its objective existence.

The New International Version states that faith is a kind of confidence for what is hoped for that furnishes assurance of a first father god. Humans hope there is a first father god and faith is the only evidence and assurance for what is not seen of it. A first father god will never be seen objectively as it does not exist outside of the imagining human brain. A human-like god is located and exists only as a subjective idea inside the human brain.

Lacking objective evidence while promoting the subjective idea of a first father god, influences a great many gullible people to accept the false concept, and is at a minimum unethical, to say the least. More accurately, to act in such a rash and irresponsible way is to commit the harm of a criminal fraud on the public.

The material facts of a human beginning is not a first father god but the evidential act of sexual procreation while supported by the earth and solar environments. There also exist the material facts of fossil artifacts of evolution of humans from earlier species of hominins.

Monotheistic authorities ignore the material facts of human origin and instead knowingly and intentionally promote the fraudulent view of a first father god for which no convincing material evidence exists.

The charge of fraud must be leveled against monotheistic authority that has and continues to knowingly and intentionally misrepresent the origin of the environment and humans to be a first father god. No evidence exists for this assertion except meager tradition and unsubstantial faith.

There is a chance, due to the vagaries of the legal system, monotheistic authorities will not be found guilty of criminal charges by the imposed criteria of a finding of guilt beyond a reasonable doubt. If this scenario occurs, civil charges must then be filed as prosecution based upon a preponderance of evidence is easier to prove. Both criminal and civil trials must be brought through the court system against prevailing leaders of the major monotheistic religions of Judaism, Christianity, and Islam.

If failing more stringent criminal prosecution and consequent conviction, incarceration or probation, at least civil monetary penalties commensurate to the harm and damage inflicted on the innocent and naïve must be heavily imposed upon monotheistic authority figures and the religions they represent. Those who advocate, promote, and perpetuate the fraud of monotheism must be held accountable and justice served.

A civil suit against monotheistic religions must be brought so as to recover monetary damages for the proffered and promoted delusion and its consequent inestimable pain and suffering inflicted by the blatant pandering and advocating of false protection by a first father god. The suit should also cite the intentional impairment of human comprehension for financial gain over many years. There is sometimes a long road of travel to finally arrive at the outcome of legal truth.

The false and deceptive view of monotheism and those who promote it must be held legally accountable and liable for the many grievous disappointments and sufferings it has inflicted upon humankind.

For the many minions who accept the imaginary view of monotheistic authorities, a monetary fine and mandatory sentence of education might also be imposed to require study of psychology, philosophy, and physics. The individual monetary fines collected can be deposited in a fund and utilized to finance a multitude of worthy charitable real human endeavors.

A final legal indictment must also be brought forward against monotheistic religious leaders. In the future, monotheism will be correctly assessed and judged to be a greater crime against humanity. Monotheistic religion can and must be charged with committing "crimes against humanity," generally defined as acts of force or aggression against members of a population. While war crimes occur during armed conflict, crimes against humanity are committed both during times of war and times of peace by a de facto authority in a systematic persecution of one group by another in a population.

Crimes against humanity consist of inhumane behaviors such as dehumanization, slavery, massacres, genocide or extermination, military use of children, experimentation on humans, and other crass and criminal behaviors. The wicked acts are not directed to a single or a few individuals but include many in a widespread practice.

A criminal act occurs when monotheistic authorities subjectively skew the origin of existence away from the environment, and instead proffer and pander the idea of a first father god. Leaders of monotheistic religions actively promote the idea that a first father god is objectively real. The de facto authority or governing groups of monotheistic religions have committed widespread coercion, cruelty, persecution, punishment, torture, imprisonment, and executions in a systematic manner. The criminal, civil, and crimes against humanity charges brought against monotheistic institutions of authority, is that they intentionally misrepresent human origin.

By so doing they cause grievous harm by falsely identifying the origin of existence to be a first father god, and by inducing a false sense of security and protection.

Individual humans like to think that someone cares for their life, and that life has some meaning as to why they exist. Therefore, many superstitious individuals readily and gullibly accept the deceptive words of monotheistic authorities who promote an imagined and caring first father god. In reality, each individual depends only on his own cerebral cortex of the brain and that of others for the idea of a numerical first father as a subjective and imagined way of denoting the genealogical descent of many biological forefathers.

Conclusion

In stark contrast to the artistically imagined and inverted biblical Garden of Eden story, the curse of life came billions of years prior to a first father god that was only much later imagined in the evolved cerebral cortex of the monotheistic word artist brain.

A first father god is an orientation to prevent disorientation in life by imagining the beginning of existence to be human-like. By imagining a first father to exist, individual adherents are prone to take chances and to risk life and limb as the god is portrayed as caring and can provide protection. A make believe first father is an artistic and imaginative way to give worth to life as a response to the often disorienting failures and less than worthwhile experiences of sadness and sorrows.

To praise a first father god is to praise the cerebral cortex of the human brain. The real basis of monotheistic religion is the cerebral cortex that imagines the beginning of existence to be a first father god. The cerebral cortex has evolved an ability to make picture images with which to both imagine and reason about past, now, and future times. While the evolved ability for picture images of time scenes and imagining and reasoning are a higher evolved development, it is not the animating essence that evolves human life.

In the writings of monotheistic religions, humans are made by a good first father god who will resurrect the body that lacks a soul. In modern folk thinking, humans do have a soul and the god will save it. Both views are completely false as the soul is a continuation of the environment and is saved not by an imagined god but by default.

The essence of the environment and earth are elements of energy, and the essence of the total seen and unseen moving universe is a cosmological force that ever exists on its own. The essence of life is a continuation of force and energy and is therefore resistant to destruction. The essence of life is the phenomenon of an animating triune soul that forces life to live and to survive, as a forcible hunger for food, sex and reproduction, and aggression.

In monotheistic religions, human attention is directed to the good of a first father god so the soulless body can be resurrected.
The real task is to learn about the good of reducing the destruction resistant soul of the body so it will not be saved, and to thereby prevent it from making a circular return to the earth to struggle through another lifetime.

The animating triune soul saves an individual who is also rescued by another natural dimension. An earthly dimension exists and therefore other dimensions are just as likely to exist. A monotheistic first father god is a mere mental artistic image utilized to escape to good from the bad potential and real suffering of life and death.

Unfortunately, the greater number of humankind will continue to accept confusing yet comforting tales of an imagined first father god and a body resurrection, or the more popular view of a good human soul. Passing through future centuries, the obscuring fog that is monotheism will slowly dissipate to eventually reveal the bright light of day. Humankind will surely progress toward and will eventually accept what is sensible and found to be true as supported by the evidence of observation, reasoning, and science. At some future time, humankind will accept the God-Soul Theory of partial-atheism, the view that a first father god is only subjectively real as an artistic imagining by word artists, and is not objectively real.

Despite the fact that monotheistic religions and modern empirical science find no evidence of an animating soul, pending future investigation, humankind will eventually come to accept that there is a triune soul resistant to destruction. There will come to be future acceptance that the soul is not a shining special presence made by an imagined ancestor first father god.

The day will surely come when the animating soul will be recognized for what it truly is, a forcible hunger for food, sex and reproduction, and aggression. The triune soul will be also be recognized to be a continuation of the energy of the earth and a real cosmological force that is beginingless and endless, and that ever exists on its own to continuously move the universe.

www.ingramcontent.com/pod-product-compliance
Lightning Source LLC
Chambersburg PA
CBHW070916270326
41927CB00011B/2590